J.D. Calvert

i

**TABLE OF CONTENTS**

| | |
|---|---|
| 2 | PREFACE |
| | PACE YOURSELF |
| | AND / OR |
| 3 | INTRODUCTION |
| 4 | ABOUT THE AUTHOR |
| 5 | MERRY CHRISTMAS TO THE MADRIGALS OF '84 |
| 5 | TO A SPECIAL PERSON IN THE CHOIR |
| 6 | ACRONYM LIST |
| 7 | CHAPTER 1. THE FIRST SEASON |
| 8 | MAD BATTERS '84, BAD ATTITUDES 0 |
| 9 | HE'LL GET OVER IT -- HE'S STILL YOUNG |
| 10 | CHAPTER 2. THE SECOND SEASON |
| 11 | TEAM CAPTAIN'S ESSAY ON PERSPECTIVE |
| 12 | UP, UP AND AWAY |
| 13 | CAPTION CONTEST FIRST PRIZE |
| 14 | MAKIN' A MOVE ON TUSCON |
| 15 | SO WHAT ELSE IS NEW |
| 15 | THE SPOILERS ARE COMING |
| 16 | TALK TO YOUR CAPTAIN: |
| 16,17 | MAD BATTER TEAM DATA FOR VIDEO UNIT |
| 18 | TEAM DATA FOR GOING DOWN AGAIN |
| 19 | THE MONDAY AFTER / SUE MAY BE THE BEST PITCHER WE HAVE |
| 20 | GOING DOWN AGAIN, WHAT A CLEVER NAME |
| 20 | MAD BATTERS '85, BAD ATTITUDES 0 |
| 21 | CHAPTER FPA. FOCAL PLANE ARRAYS AND OTHER SHIT |
| 21 | TIME FOR A DRIBBLE FROM THE PIPELINE |
| 22 | IT'S GOOD BUT IT COULD BE BETTER |
| 22 | NO SWEAT !! |
| 23 | THE "*I AIN' T GOT NO DETECTOR*" BLUES |
| 24 | IT AIN'T OVER 'TIL IT'S OVER |
| 24 | THE LABS ARE EMPTY BUT THE CONFERENCE ROOMS ARE FULL |
| 25 | THE *I AIN'T GOT NO DETECTOR* BLUES... REPRISE |
| 26 | OUTTA HERE |
| 26 | I TOLD YOU SO |
| 27 | CHAPTER 3. THE THIRD SEASON |
| 27 | GET WELL QUICK, SUE'S KNEEDED |
| 28 | LOSERS CAN BE WINNERS TOO |
| 28 | THESE CLOSE CALLS ARE WEARING ME OUT |
| 29 | THE TUESDAY AFTER |
| 30, 31 | MAD BATTER DATA FOR VIDEO UNIT |
| 33 | MULE & THE GANG DATA FOR VIDEO UNIT |
| 34, 35 | SNATCHING POETRY FROM THE JAWS OF DEFEAT |
| 36 | THE TUESDAY AFTER |
| 37 | WHOA!  ROAD APPLES ON THE TRAIL |
| 37 | WELCOME TO C-3 LEAGUE |

| | |
|---|---|
| 38 | THE MONDAY AFTER |
| 39 | TALK TO YOUR CAPTAIN |
| 40 | OBOY, THE FINAL '86 SEASON NEWSLETTER |
| 40 | MAD BATTERS '86, BAD ATTITUDES 0 |
| 41 | MAD ABOUT THIS CHRISTMAS PARTY |
| 42 | DARN!  ONLY 12 MONTHS THIS YEAR |
| 42 | A CLASS ACT, NO MATTER WHAT HAND HE'S DEALT |
| 42 | PROPOSAL PRAYER |
| 43 | RED TEAM BLUES |
| 44 | SAMPLES PER DWELL |
| 44 | A YEAR'S END MUSE |
| 45 | ALAS POOR YORK, WE KNEW HIM WELL |
| 46 | NO SHIT |
| 46 | VERSE 2: A CLASS ACT |
| 47 | CHAPTER 4.   THE '87 SEASON |
| 48 | IT'S ONLY A(NOTHER) GAME |
| 49 | ON BEING 8-0 IN C2 LEAGUE |
| 50 | IS IT TOO LATE TO MAKE OUR MOVE? |
| 50 | AWSHIT, WE WON ONE |
| 51 | THE MONDAY AFTER |
| 52 | IT'S BEEN FUN TO KNOW YOU |
| 52 | YOU'RE OKAY IF I'M UPWIND |
| 53 | THE TUESDAY AFTER |
| 54 | MAD BATTERS '87, BAD ATTITUDES 0 |
| 55 | SOUND EFFECTS |
| 55 | I CHOSE THE WRONG CURTAIN AND I GOT ZONKED |
| 56 | HEY, LIGHTEN UP; IT'S NOT HAPPENING TO ME |
| 57 | WHAT'S A NICE KID LIKE YOU … ? |
| 58 | A SHORT POEM FOR YOUR BIRTHDAY |
| 58 | ANOTHER JOAN POEM |
| 58 | SHORT NOTICE |
| 59 | HEY, IT'S ONLY A JOB WELL DONE |
| 59 | SHORT REFRAIN |
| 60 | SHE WENT THATAWAY |
| 60 | TAKE A NUMBER |
| 60 | PERIODIC POETRY |
| 61 | PAUL'S POEM |
| 61 | THE DARTS JUST BOUNCE OFF |
| 62 | ODE TO ELI |
| 62 | OFF THE MARK |
| 63 | SAY "PHYSICIST"--(Gesundheit !) |
| 64 | CHAPTER 5. THE '88 SEASON |
| 65 | CHAPTER 6. THE '89 SEASON |
| 66 | ANCIENT HISTORY |
| 66 | HAPPY BIRTHDAY LADY !!! |
| 66 | HEY, YOU COULD PASS FOR 38 ANY DAY |

| | |
|---|---|
| 67 | WEATHER GOEST? |
| 67 | ANOTHER GOOD DEED GONE WRONG |
| 67 | HAPPY BIRTHDAY BARBARA (HOW OLD?) |
| 68 | STILL ON FIRE |
| 68 | AUGUST BODIES |
| 68 | UNBELIEVABLE FOR HIS AGE |
| 69 | HAPPY BIRTHDAY TO MS. X |
| 69 | HOT DAMN |
| 70 | YUPPIE BLUES |
| 70 | HAPPY BIRTHDAY PUMPKIN HEADS |
| 70 | MERRY BIRTHDAY |
| 71 | CHAPTER 7. THE SEVENTH SEASON |
| 72 | HOT DAMN WE ALMOST WON A BIG ONE |
| 73 | FANTASTIC FINAL GAME TEAM |
| 73 | SO MANY PITCHES, SO LITTLE TIME |
| 74 | MOVING POETRY |
| 74 | CREW BLUE |
| 75 | SHIPSHAPE !!! |
| 76 | THEY MADE IT AGAIN |
| 76 | FLIGHT 708 |
| 76 | STEPPED IN WHAT? |
| 77 | JUNE IS BUSTING OUT ALL OVER |
| 77 | BE THERE !?! |
| 78 | THE MAD BATTERS |

*********************************************************************

| | |
|---|---|
| 79 | GOT XMAS? |
| 79 | MAD OR MERRY: WHAT'S THE DIFFERENCE? |
| 80 – 97 | XMAS POEMS PAST |

*********************************************************************

| | |
|---|---|
| 98 | GOT 80 ??? |
| 99 | ANCIENT HISTORY, PART 1 |
| 99 | T + 4,560,080 AND COUNTING |
| 99 | ANCIENT HISTORY, PART 2 |
| 100 | ENJOYING IRRELEVANCE   or   NOT QUITE DEAD YET |
| 101 | GOT MILK? |

*********************************************************************

| | |
|---|---|
| 102 | MOMS & DADS |
| 103 | HAPPY MOTHER'S DAY !!! |
| 103 | HAPPY FATHER'S DAY !!! |

*********************************************************************

| | |
|---|---|
| 105 | A POEM TOO FAR? |
| 106,107 | A POEM TOO FAR?  or  CAN I BE IN THE DEAD POET'S SOCIETY NOW? |
| 107 | A(NOTHER) FINAL POEM |

# Aerospace Softball

by

## J.D. Calvert

ISBN 978-0-578-67896-2

## PREFACE

A few words-o-caution seem called for:

## PACE YOURSELF

Some of my poems are simple to read:
    The beat is smooth and lazy.
        Many of the others
           require quite a bit of effort:
              finding the rhythm just makes you crazy!?!

## AND / OR

I've polished this poetry over and over
    -- it's driving me 'round the bend ! --
    '    Alas there are so many syllables to consider
        that I fear it will / wonder will it / never end !?!

*WOW! THAT WAS SURE A BAD EARTHQUAKE!*

## INTRODUCTION

This book is primarily a collection of smart-ass poems and newsletter "highlights" generated in honor of the Mad Batters, a coed slow-pitch softball team. I think the Mad Batters' reverence for this game was best captured by my teammate, Wiley, who observed that, "Most of the players on this team think softball is a venereal disease!" Nonetheless, after seven seasons of fierce competition, the Mad Batters were firmly wedged in the middle of the lowest softball league (C-3) -- that is, 33rd out of the 36 teams sponsored by the Wonderful Aerospace Corporation (WAC) in Southern California. Accordingly -- figuring that we'd about peaked -- I thought it was important to share the Mad Batters' message with the entire free world. ....Well okay, the poems won't rhyme unless you read English and your vocabulary includes the words "fart" and "shit". But that's not all.

## ABOUT THE AUTHOR

On our *Crown Princess* cruise in 2010 one of the ports-o-call was Norfolk, VA where we docked next to the Naval Nautical Museum featuring *USS Wisconsin BB64*. This was *alma mater* for my first midshipman cruise summer '57: Norfolk to Valpariso, Chile via the Panama Canal and return. Thankfully *Wisconsin* was the best ocean ride *ever* so Dave didn't barf at all, and the USN didn't discover that problem until my summer '59 cruise aboard a destroyer ...... *boy* did they discover that problem!!! By then the Navy had so much inve$ted in me (full NROTC scholarship) that they adopted a "Don't ask, don't tell" approach and let me graduate ... tho' they were careful to put me aboard a ship that pretty much stayed in drydock at Portsmouth VA !

An Engineering Physicist by education, electro-optical system analyst by profession and sailor by passion -- well okay, not so much "sailor" as "boater", inasmuch as 98% of his sea stories have to do with outboard engine problems --   Jack David was always the last one chosen for athletic teams as a youth, and his athletic skills got even worse with age. Furthermore, until 1981 David confined his "poetry" to the usual family Christmas ditty:

> Again this year we're running late;
> That always seems to be our fate.
> So much to do, so little time,
> And now we're stuck with this damn rhyme!
>     etc.

In October of 1981, however, he launched (via crane over his roof) a 28' catamaran he'd built in his backyard and garage, and he began to exhibit other symptoms of *dain bramage* in the form of "poems" and caption contests related to his work in the aerospace industry. Perhaps these smart-ass works were mental counterweights to the numerous technical engineering proposals and reports he helped prepare. Or perhaps he was inspired by the fun and magic people he worked with, and he seeks hereby to honor them and share their delightful personalities with a wider audience.      ...... Nah! He probably just needed some money to support his boating habit and hoped to sell this to a publisher.   In any case, he sincerely hopes you have as much fun reading this book as he had writing it !!

4

## MERRY CHRISTMAS TO THE MADRIGALS OF '84

Here's to the magic Madrigal Singers of Edison High School:
        Your singing is *fantastic*, and your looks are really cool.
                A lot of your success, of course, is also Mr. Otey's;
                        I think the guy could get harmony
                                from a pack of wild coyotes!
And when you're not on stage you throw
        a party that's really great;
                I only hope you don't get a lot of gas
                        from the ton of food you ate.
You'll always look back proudly
        on these years when your voices grew.
                I wish you continued happiness,
                        and may all of your dreams come true!


## TO A SPECIAL PERSON IN THE CHOIR

Your voice is weak and whiny,
        you hardly ever know your part,
                And when we sing *pianissimo*
                        everyone can hear you fart!

### ACRONYM LIST

I have tried to keep the number of acronyms used herein to an absolute minimum, but acronyms are an inescapable part of aerospace literature, and so I have necessarily included the ones explained here.

**A.S.S. Air-to-Surface Seeker**
This is WAC's latest project, a sophisticated missile that is guided by an imaging infrared sensor. The heart of this sensor is its focal plane array of infrared detectors. These need a lot more development, but so far, even with the present FPAs, this missile has successfully sought the surface every time it was launched from the air!

**BAC    Bad Aerospace Corporation**
This is the competition, and I would accuse them of being ogres and sex deviates if so many of them weren't us and vice versa; that is, there is a lot of transient labor in the aerospace industry.   One thing for sure is that when (all too often) BAC beats us out of a big contract it is because they have somehow cheated!   We spend a lot of time trying to figure out their secrets of success.

**FPA    Focal Plane Array**
This is a little tiny chip containing thousands of itsy-bitsy detector elements. On a good day (or night) these detectors can turn a rain of millions of infrared photons into a corresponding stream of electrons which spray out (eventually) onto a television screen and produce a very expensive picture.

**$I^2R$    Imaging Infrared or FLIR**
Like television but sees in the dark.   Usually the only program you can get is some clown drinking coffee and leaving his warm hand print on his pants.    If you're lucky he may also light a match.

**MTF   Modulation Transfer Function**
A measure of how well an imaging sensor sees little details in the dark -- like does the clown have his fly zipped.

**MCT   merc cad telluride     mercury-cadmium-telluride**
This is the primary material used to manufacture FPAs.   If you can discover a vein of this stuff in your mine, you might become a very rich prospector.

**MAD   Mission Analysis Department**
This group contemplates the military's long term requirements and tries to get WAC into position to bid on big contracts. Their primary tool is the dart board at various Officers Clubs.

**SOBAD        Second Order Ballistic Aiming Device**
For a couple of years, this sophisticated electronic unit was the big money product for WAC's sister division. Then somebody pointed out that the troops really didn't have much use for an aiming device -- however clever -- when they tossed their hand grenades, and next thing we knew the darn program got cancelled!   (But not before there was a lot of nasty press.)

**WAC  Wonderful Aerospace Corporation**
Somebody has to wear the white hats, and in the aerospace industry WAC got the job. WAC is wonderfully organized: at the top of the heap, so to speak, are engineers-turned-bean-counters and at the bottom is an unruly mob of technical-types who are never happy with any of the decisions handed down to them and could care less about the beans.

## CHAPTER 1. THE FIRST SEASON

In 1984 the Wonderful Aerospace Corporation (acronym: WAC), reinstated a softball program that had been dormant for a decade. In the intervening years this game had somehow changed. On the good side, it was now coed: at least two ladies had to be on the field at all times (and there were now 10 players on the defense with the addition of a roving fielder). On the bad side (for my money) the game had become "slow pitch":   To be declared a *strike* the ball had to be lobbed in an arc that peaked at a height of between 6 and 12 feet and then descend to actually strike the rubber of home plate -- which was now enlarged to 17" x 34". Short-sighted umpires must have thought this one up; not only was this pitch hard to deliver (the Mad Batters were always hurting in the pitching department), but also I considered it harder to hit (although I managed to do so about half the time).

Of course no one asked me for my opinion, what with my legendary athletic skills and all. So I was pleased and proud to accept an invitation by my supervisor (he picked the nickname "Bones" for reasons no one has ever deciphered) to join the Department slow-pitch softball team.   I chose to overlook the fact that there were only 13 people in our department. About half of the team's members were young men who could accurately be described as jocks, but the other half of us were more than able to overcome this handicap.

In addition to selecting our own nickname (emblazoned on our Jersey) we democratically chose a team name (I voted for *Master Batters*) and became the

*Mad Batters.*

The Mad Batters had some success in the qualifying games (even beating the Loggers!), but we were consigned to the lowest league (C-2 that year) together with 9 other teams of seemingly similar talents; the Loggers were understandably pissed at having been dragged into this league by our inadvertent win.   At that point Bones feigned too busy a schedule (although he still played nearly every game) and turned the team over to the newest hire in our section, John ("JC"), who also happened to be an excellent ballplayer and (fortunately, as it turned out) had a delightfully fatalistic sense of humor.

As the season unfolded it became apparent the Mad Batters were not going to lead the league.   In fact, except for a couple of practice games against Going Down Again, we somehow lost every game in the regular season, and only beat the Hot Dogs in the "playoff" because their team had been even more decimated by injury and desertion than the Mad Batters.

Upon our loss of game number 4 (ironically, to the Hot Dogs), I became inspired to generate a "poem" to our efforts... and then another... and another...

## MAD BATTERS '84, BAD ATTITUDES 0

I think we peaked too early
    -- we beat the Loggers in the quals --
        'Cause from then on it was all downhill
           -- in fact it was over the falls !

## HE'LL GET OVER IT--HE'S STILL YOUNG

Here's to JC the Coach: we'll never forget him.
    Who'd think such a nice guy's chances
        of winning were so slim ?!?
After all: the Mad Batters had *some* talent
    of which he might happily gloat,
        ... Nonetheless Coach told me he'd like just once
          to get his hands around Bones's throat!
Or at least he'd like to *thank* Bones
    for giving him this team;
        It fulfilled every expectation
          of his most-horrible-ever dream.
Tightly clutching the backstop,
    Coach'd see the offense muff hit after hit,
        And from his position in far left field he'd watch
          our crack defensive unit turn to shit!
But these nightmares are all *his*
    -- to be locked forever
        deep down in his mind's vault --
          While the rest of the team sleeps easy,
            'cause we know it was the Coach's fault!

CHAPTER 2. THE SECOND SEASON

In late '84 and early '85 several of the original Mad Batters (alas, the younger, better ball players) changed jobs and went to work for arch rival Bad Aerospace Company (BAC). It probably had nothing to do with our "winning" season.   As the '85 softball season approached I chanced to inquire of the Mad Batters' leader, JC, as to when we would begin practice?   He responded by announcing that he was retiring from softball, and suggested that *I* might like to take over the Mad Batters' reins!?! Well the whole thing had been far too fun to abandon, so I accepted the offer and set off to recruit the necessary replacements.

In my recruiting drive I was at pains to point out that the overridingly important requirement for membership on our team was an enthusiasm for Fun without regard for softball skills.   Guess what?   I had very little trouble getting a team back together!   In the first place, the young Jocks who had quit were replaced by two equally athletic young engineers, and I let them believe it was their *duty* to join the Department softball team.   I was also able to recruit five new ladies for our team since only June had survived the off season "cuts". (There was some gossip to the effect that I overly enjoyed this lady recruiting business.)   Best of all, at the last minute JC decided to remain with the team and even agreed to act as player-coach -- so long as absolutely no paperwork was involved.

Thus the Mad Batters' staff was abundantly replenished as we set off on the new '85 pre-season practices and games.   In my new, more responsible -- albeit no more knowledgeable -- role as Team Captain I followed JC's lead and adopted a newsletter format to publish the vital team information that appears here -- but don't get your hopes too high: there are still plenty of poems embedded too!

## TEAM CAPTAIN'S ESSAY ON PERSPECTIVE
### ( for MAD BATTER eyes only!?! )

1. The goal is for everyone to play and have fun.

2. Winning is nice but not worth killing for or getting hurt.

3. Playing on this team will NOT lead to a contract
        in professional slow-pitch softball.

4. In this league there are a lot of errors: DO YOUR PART !!

5. As a result of #4 above:   If in doubt -- GO FOR IT !!
        -- Hitting, running bases, throwing, catching, drinking!

6. Other key features of Mad Batter style softball:

    o A proper slide into first base can turn even the wimpiest hit
            into an easy single.

    o No ball is hit so high over your head that you can't reach it
            by throwing your glove.

    o Don't get discouraged if the enemy team seems to be pulling ahead
            -- they're also getting tired faster.

    o Proper execution of the Mad Batter Shuffle
            can turn even the best enemy offense into mush!

    o There is never any doubt when it comes time to decide
            whether to play one more inning
                    or to head for Post Game Attitude Adjustment.

UP, UP AND AWAY

Once upon a time there was a ball team
         with a very tall Mad Batter;
                  Sadly for us all next year
                           we'll have the former but not the latter.
'Cause Art's leaving WAC to try out
         BAC's swamp in Seal Beach,
                  And tho' we'll miss him here,
                           we wish him well
                                    in his search for new heights to reach.
But what about poor Harold:
         now who can he look up to?
                  And who'll be there when we need someone
                           to chug a pitcher of beer or two?
Grow up Art; your leaving
         is really shortsighted and bad!
                           How can you give up on a company
                                    that makes a product line called SOBAD?
And it's more than a little tacky to split
         right after winning the contest first prize
                  For a smart-ass cheeky caption
                           (attached right here before your eyes).
But then again as I recall,
         he greeted the prize with mixed emotion
                           -- Something about hangovers combined with catamarans
                                    and trips upon the ocean.
So here's to Art: a helluva nice guy;
         For his quality work he should be paid a bounty.
                  Although he'll be gone, you can still spot his shadow:
                           it's the one that spans all of Orange County!

MAKIN' A MOVE ON TUSCON

Steve is on the move again;
     his ass is out the door.
          We'll miss him at the ball games
               and at the parties even more!
But BAC has made him an offer
     to be a part-time professional student,
          And if you can get a deal such as that,
               *take it!* if you're wise and prudent.
BAC has even assured him
     that he'll still be near the beach ....
          … Never mind the Gila monsters
               and the cattle bones left to bleach.
Never mind as well the girls
     with skin tanned the texture of the bark of trees;
          You wouldn't kiss them anyway
               since 9 out of 10 have herpes.
And while we're listing some negatives,
     don't forget the Apaches are surly;
          They're still pissed off about their land,
               and their favorite scalps are curly.
Of course there are some good things too,
     and I'd list them both if I could,
          But I'm all choked up about his leaving
               so my memory's not too good.
Adios to the guy we've all come to like
     in the short time that we've worked with him;
          To the guy who once couldn't spell SOBAD
               -- and even today his chances seem slim.
Adios to the guy who's decent and kind
     and wears his heart upon his sleeve;
          Who, when asked for a clever nickname
               to put on his Mad Batters jersey,
                    without hesitation replied, "Steve" !

## SO WHAT ELSE IS NEW

Its not as inspiring to win, win, win
         -- Especially from Going Down Aga
                    i
                   n
                   (again);
Although notable boozers, They're known to be losers.

## THE SPOILERS ARE COMING

Despite enormous talent, our team is five and oh*;
     With the exception of the Loggers,
     no other team has that record to show!
So it's with definite mixed emotions
     that I watch these next days pass,
        'Cause when we meet Going Down Aga
                  i
                 n
                 (again)
         we'll (as usual) kick ' em in the A.S.S

---

*Well okay, it's really 0 and 5, but that version is depressing, and besides it doesn't rhyme!

15

TALK TO YOUR CAPTAIN:
*Question*:     Does the official Mad Batter uniform have to include a bra?
*Answer*:     No.          Definitely not.          Hell no !!
              …. And we're begging you, Wiley: PLEASE STOP !!!

POSTLUDE: Since, as Scruffy noted upon finishing his second slice of free pizza and washing it down with our beer, "there ain't no video", it is only fair to publish here some *Mad Batter* and *Going Down Again* biographical data that your captain prepared for our crack video unit.

MAD BATTER TEAM DATA FOR VIDEO UNIT

1. *John (Rover, Left)*.   Lead off batter "JC" had .533 average last year and was the team captain. Demoted to Coach this year because he allowed a win to creep into an otherwise perfect Mad Batter season last year. John not only captained / coached last year, but also he created the Mad Batter logo, started the newsletter, and set up the statistics forms that we are using again this year.

2. *Sue (Pitcher, First Base)*.   "Screwball Sue" is new to the team this year but is one of our top players and can handle any position. She has had a checkered past, and it would be interesting to know what she considered to be the highlight(s) of it all? Perhaps the stint at the Harley-Davidson factory?

3. *Brad (Shortstop, Rover)*.   Brad is also new to the team this year. He is, however, an excellent player having learned almost everything about the game from his office mate, Wiley.   Brad is also the team hunk, of which you may want to ask him more.   Or you could ask some of the ladies on the team.

4. *Ralph (Pitcher)*. "Rabid Ralph" pitched a lot for us last year too, and he batted an incredible .778.    He is famous for his "minimum energy trajectory" style base running and was almost run down on the baseline last week as a result. Ralph is faking a foot injury this week because he has a kinky idea of what a "pinch runner" is all about.

5. *Mark (Left, Rover)*.   Mark is new to the team this year. He is the home run king to date, however, having belted two big ones last week. He is also no slouch in the "hunk" department, as your cross-examinations may well discover.

6. *Chris (Second)*.   Chris comes to us from SOBAD, but we have forgiven her because she is an excellent ballplayer. She is the team smoker -- we are an equal opportunity ball team -- and should be asked how she plans to spend her summer (hint: Here Comes the Bride).

7. *Darrell (Short, Rover, Pitcher)*. "Gramps" batted .523 last year and has played his usual high energy game again this year. There is no truth to the rumor that the number on his Jersey (82) is his age this year, but you may want to check it out.

8. *Judy (Second).* New to the team this year. Judy is an excellent ballplayer, and we are all real nice to her because she is in Contracts! Judy likes our team because we do not discriminate on the basis of your legs. (We accepted Wiley for example). Ask her!

9. *Henry (Third).* "Shoe" batted .538 last year. Henry's jobs on the team are to (a) try to find us each week both before and after the game, and (b) to RBI Judy who bats ahead of him. Rotsa ruck, Hank!

10. *June (Right, Catcher).* Batted .154 last year but has been to the batting cages this year, so we expect great things. June plays a lead role in cheering us up at Post Game Attitude Adjustment as well.

11. *Wiley (Right, Catcher).* New to us from SOBAD, but before that he was a valued member of the WAC team with Ralph, David, et al. Wiley has taught Brad almost everything he knows about the game, and his skills are second only to the Team Captain's.

12. *Betty (Catcher, Right).* New to the team this year but learning fast! Betty has a lot of the Mad Batter go-for-it spirit, and her main goal in this game is to outshine her sister Mary who plays for the enemy team. (We had an option on Mary during pre-season play, but had to sell her to Going Down Again as we were already staffed up).

13. *Dave (First Base).* "Bones" batted .400 last year but was the originator of the Mad Batters last year. He never seems to stop smirking about how he was able to get this team started and then hand it off to John before the shit hit the fan. Ask Bones if his kleptomania is getting better (but don't let him hold the mic when he answers). P.S. Bones choreographed the Mad Batter Shuffle!??!

14. Jill *(Catcher, Right).* New to the team this year and was one of the few people in America who had never even heard of this game until she was recruited for the Mad Batters. We still haven't found the loophole in our brochure …

15. *Jerry (Center).* Jerry was a reluctant recruit this year but has played well although he seems injury prone; the others on the team are hoping the gods have singled out Jerry for attack and will be kind to the rest of us.

16. *Jack David (Third).* Team Captain this year -- John didn't seem too sorry to transfer the reins -- and batted a surprising .565 last year. At third base *The Mouth* is generally recognized as the loudest weak spot in C-3 League: "*Close your eyes and hit toward the sound*" has been the advice of most opposing coaches.

17. *Russ (Center).* New to the team this year and formerly with BAC. We were all pleasantly surprised to learn that Russ is a world-class sprinter. This should definitely give us an edge, and we have been careful to put him in the lineup behind Team Captain to keep Russ from burning himself out on the baseline.

## TEAM DATA FOR GOING DOWN AGAIN

These people are known losers, but here is the little data I could find on them. The data -- like their game plan -- is in no particular order.

*Tom (#69, Pitcher).* "Souz" is a nice guy but no way a pitcher. The way it probably happened was that someone said, "Can you be the pitcher?", and he thought they said, "Can you pee a pitcher?", so he said, "Sure if you're buying!".

*Leo (#69, First base).* "Fur Ball" was selected for first base because he is good at standing in one place. His other defensive skill is an extremely offensive vocabulary which he shares with any baserunner who has to stop at first.

*Jim (#69, Center field).* "Huh?" is Going Down Again's team captain. He earns his nickname over and over. We suspect he has Mafia connections because he always gets a better deal on pizza for his team than we can.

*Mark I (#69, Third base).* I have to watch what I say about this first Mark (they have two on their team) because a lot of people think he plays third base somewhat like I do.

*Mark II (#69, Wherever).* His furry brother Leo taught Mark II everything he knows about the game, so Mark II doesn't know shit !

*Sid (#69, Left Field).* We have always suspected that Sid is a ringer and plays professional slow-pitch softball on the weekends; he is way too good to be playing on this team for no pay!

*Mike (#69, Shortstop).* "Zonk" (see below) thinks "Mikey" has real nice physical attributes. Mikey is also too good for this team; ask how much they pay him!

*Ron (#69, Right field).* Nobody knows where this guy came from; he is just a body they scraped up to fill out their roster today, thinking we would all go sailing and give them an easy forfeit.

*Carol (#69, Catcher).* Just another body!!!!!

*Dori Ann ( #69, Third base).* "Zonk" scouts professional slow-pitch teams on the weekends; mostly she looks in the singles bars. She is playing with a sore throat and other imagined ailments today; our game plan is to hit to her a lot!

*Mary Jane (#69, 2nd base).* Watch out, this team not only has two Marks, but also they have two Marys! I'm betting she made this name up herself!

*Mary Beth (#69, Catcher).* Mary Beth is Betty's -- of the Mad Batters -- sister. Mary Beth was voted Strike-Out Queen of C-3 League in a recent poll, but she never gives up and is more than good enough for this team!

6-10-85   THE MONDAY AFTER …

Well it's always frustrating to lose a big one, especially after you've invested so much time and effort getting ready for it; then, when you blow it bad -- even after your best execution of the game plan -- it is really a terribly depressing experience.   But enough about our crack video unit, let's talk about the *Mad Batters'* second big win of the season, against *Going Down Again*; final score 22-12 !?!   This week we've got to praise the pitching staff right up front:

\*\*\*\*\*\*\*\*\*\*\*\*\*\*\*\*\*\*\*\*\*\*\*\*\*\*\*\*\*\*\*\*\*\*\*\*\*\*\*\*\*

## SUE MAY BE THE BEST PITCHER WE HAVE

Here's to Sue the pitcher:
>      worked the whole game without relief,
>>           And brought Going Down Again
>>>                down again; they ended up in grief !!

Tho' this enemy's sick offense
>      preferred a walk instead of a hit,
>>           Sue's body-english screwball
>>>                soon turned their strategy into shit!

So she forced them to resort to hitting
>      in their incredibly wimpy style,
>>           And the way our defense handled these
>>>                was so awesome it made Sue smile.

(Except of course for your Captain
>      -- you're being kind if you call his fielding shitty --
>>           But Gramps backs up his every move
>>>                so the team's effective even tho' it ain't pretty.)

Well the net result was Mad Batter victory
>      when Souz's shove came up against Sue's push,
>>           But everyone's still wondering what she meant
>>>                by, "Don't beat around the bush?"

\*\*\*\*\*\*\*\*\*\*\*\*\*\*\*\*\*\*\*\*\*\*\*\*\*\*\*\*\*\*\*\*\*\*\*\*\*\*\*\*\*

Neither the stats nor my words (nor the video record, darn it !) can describe the power shown by our offense! HRs were belted by Gramps (2) and Mark; keep eating them Wheaties !!! Attaboys !!!!!

Brad's sister, Cindy, watched the entire game and then was overheard telling Brad, "They aren't nearly the losers you told me!" Thanks sis.

Of Bones' coverage at first base, Sue stated, "It's not so bad because most of their hits are fly outs or doubles; come to think of it, most of their singles become doubles too."

GOING DOWN AGA
                    I
                        N .... WHAT A CLEVER NAME

The Mouth sends his greetings
        and condolences in your sorrow;
                Perhaps your team's fortunes
                        will improve upon the 'morrow?
... Of course some things never change
        'tho considerable time passes,
                So I'm not really too surprised
                        that you were felled by the Asses.
And even 'tho there's a game to go
        'ere they ring down this season's curtain,
                Your place on the bottom
                        of the lowest league
                                is now essentially certain !!


MAD BATTERS '85, BAD ATTITUDES 0

Here's to the Mad Batters:
        you're a helluva a softball team!
                And a super fantastic fun bunch of people
                        -- no matter how quiet and shy you seem.
Your stats are absolutely awesome
        (you're champs no matter what anyone thinks):
                You've downed 40 pizzas, 70 pitchers of beer
                        and 10 blenders of yucca drinks!
Along the way you've lobbed 1200 slow-pitches,
        scored 147 runs on at-bats numbering 331,
                And never lost sight of the Mad Batter objective:
                        for everyone to play and have fun !!
So here's to the incredible Mad Batters;
        'twas a ball so let's do it again next year,
                But meanwhile let's concentrate on the really important stuff
                        -- like getting this party into high gear !!!

CHAPTER FPA.   FOCAL PLANE ARRAYS AND OTHER SHIT

Some of my earliest "poetry" was aimed (in *fun*, guys, honest!) at the people who design and develop the little electronic chips that detect infrared energy and allow our missiles to "see" in the dark.

This is an uncertain science, depending on dogged persistence to search for just the right chemistry and procedures to produce a reliable detector. There is absolutely no way of predicting, within a decade, when this search will find success, and each new detector design is pretty much a new ballgame, so to speak.

It is a true paradox of aerospace contracting, therefore, that the detector people must not only schedule their minor miracles but also forecast a commensurate cost.    Guess what? They are very often wrong on both counts!

Well, inasmuch as our proposed systems* count on these detectors' performance -- not to mention their existence -- I feel it is my duty to pick on our detector group without mercy! Lucky for me they are a good natured lot -- not counting, that is, the occasional appearance of noxious gases in our building's air conditioning system after the posting of a particularly acrid poem.
    *For example A.S.S. and SOBAD


TIME FOR A DRIBBLE FROM THE PIPELINE?

Greetings to the Ashlyholes from Systems
    -- you know we's really Mean! --
        we'd like delivery of a full FPA
            by Friday, December 13.
'Though we're well aware that this day
        normally carries an evil curse,
            we figure where FPAs are concerned
                our luck can't really get any worse !

## IT'S GOOD BUT IT COULD BE BETTER

Here's to McCorkle from the A.S.S.holes:
We admire your missile concept and its low cost goals.
It needs $I^2R$ to see at night,
And we believe A.S.S. does the job just right.
With this seeker's capabilities,
your missile can penetrate deep,
And it's readily affordable
-- but it won't be cheap!


## NO SWEAT !!

Hot Damn ! !
The A.S.S. holes have definitely won ! !
Who said you couldn't both succeed
and at the same time have lotsa fun.
Now there're FPA's to develop and gimbal sets
and optics that won't quit;
And tracker hardware and tracker software
and all kinds of other shit.
Our seeker's gonna give the missile
one helluva nice smooth ride
With "eyes" -- Ashlyholes willing --
of merc cad telluride.
But don't forget to keep it cheap:
AFFORDABLE is the goal
Because after we pay for this fantastic party
we'll be in a deep financial hole.
... Or at least that's the fiscal goal
for which we all are sworn to strive,
If only -- with sufficient Geritol --
our aged A.S.S.-holes stay alive.
And when (after 20 years of production)
the A.S.S. flag is finally furled,
They'll simply donate the thing
(tattered and torn though it be)
to the A.S.S. wing of Leisure World !!

THE "*I AIN' T GOT NO DETECTOR*" BLUES
(To the Tune of Home On the Range)*

Picture this (what a spectre),
　　　All systems GO -- but no detector!
　　　　　A crime you say? Not so fast:
　　　　　　　This same offense has made BAC vast.
　　　　　　　　　Their profits swell as follow-ons flow
　　　　　　　　　　　With the same requirement:
　　　　　　　　　　　　　"Another half way go".
Hey what about WAC -- we're not there either --
　　　so give us a contract; we need a breather
　　　　　from in-house funding (which ain't that great,
　　　　　　　especially with SOBAD eating most of the plate.
　　　　　　　　　… Perhaps there's a synergistic way:
　　　　　　　　　　　If SOBAD's projectile needs an FPA .... ? )
But what happens if -- I perish the thought --
　　　They build a detector that works as it ought?
　　　　　Then they take their seats -- Ashly, Mike and Filpins --
　　　　　　　To watch *Systems* do its twists, twirls and spins.
And what if the noises aren't what we said,
　　　And 	at if our MTF's are all out of bed?
　　　　　(1 shudder to think of the arrows and spears!
　　　　　　　Oh god how we'll long for the "Good Old Years".)
So mark my words (they're finally running slim):
　　　Tho' our present sensor's "eyes" are dim,
　　　　　It may be better (after all things pass)
　　　　　　　Than having our Systems head up its A.S.S. !

---

*Good Luck

## IT AIN'T OVER 'TIL IT'S OVER

In '82 the message was simple and mean:
    "Good detectors are few and far between."
        Sneakier in '83:
            "What a spectre, All systems GO -- but no detector!"
Upbeat in '84:   "A.S.S taking a ride
    with eyes -- Ashlyholes willing -- of merc cad telluride."
        Now here we are in '85,
            Our hopes are dimmer but still alive,
And the Wonderful Aerospace crack detector team
    (Oops! a poor choice of words it would seem)
        Is still closing in with every passing day
            on the elusive and mysterious MCT FPA,
And they never give up,
    and they shrug off every rhyme,
        'Cause their clocks are calibrated
            in units of geological time !

## THE LABS ARE EMPTY BUT THE CONFERENCE ROOMS ARE FULL

Given that good detectors
    are few and far between
        And that there are many, many
            detector secrets left to glean
And given that it's impossible
    to schedule a technology breakthru
        And that WAC's staff
            of detector technologists is few
Then how can it be
    -- by what management quirk --
        That this staff spends more time
            at status meetings
                than they do at work?!?

## THE *I AIN'T GOT NO DETECTOR* BLUES ... REPRISE

Imagine this--what a spectre -- all systems Go but no detector!
    A crime you say?... Depends on your perspective of course:
        Could it be instead
            some planner got the cart before the horse?

After all, Jim always cautioned
    that our plans might be wildly optimistic,
        And that what we had scheduled had never been done before
            so there was no knowing what was realistic.

But he was always so *cheerful* when he said it
    that we thought he might be kidding,
        And when we asked him for the best imaginable FPA
            we forgot to ask if that went
                with the cost and schedule we were bidding.

Well, the system we envisioned was so fantastic -- had it only worked --
    it would've made national headlines.
        If only those darn detector folks
            had met our randomly chosen deadlines.

And having missed our arbitrary milestone dates
    you think they'd all be tearful,
        But when we looked in the laboratory windows
            Jim and the gang
                always seemed so depressingly *cheerful !?!*

As though they were satisfied doing the best job they could,
    making progress steadily, bit by bit;
        As though -- you don't suppose!?! --
            they always knew our schedules and costs
                were just a lot of bullshit!!!

## OUTTA HERE

Here's to the A.S.S.holes: the seeker's finally out the door!
  So, in a nostalgic mood, I re-read the proposal
    written many years before.

It now appears we may have been optimistic
  -- do the adverb "wildly" ring a bell? --
    Especially the part about "Low-Cost, Low-Risk Approach"
      and about "a High Confidence Schedule" as well.

On the other hand, WAC's the one who predicted
  "Good Detectors are Few and Far Between,"
    And we've certainly demonstrated *that* to be a fact
      so please don't treat us mean!

Besides, the progress and learning
  have been substantial in every technical respect,
    And you *can* see a long wavelength infrared image
      even though the quality is not up to spec.

Furthermore our seeker is software programmable
  -- everybody knows that's modern and good --
    I just wish it didn't require three full-time programmers
      to generate a picture that looks like it should.

So how to respond to A.S.S. critics who point out
  ADO's been dissolved and MICOM is broke?
    Say, "Picky, picky, picky" for one thing
      and then, "Screw 'em if they can't take a Joke!"


## I TOLD YOU SO

Here's to the inquisitors of A.S.S.
  They're out to decipher this incredible mess.
    It'll be complicated,
      but their result can be anticipated:
Of cartoons and rhymes there should be more
  and of technical specs there should be less !!

CHAPTER 3:   THE THIRD SEASON

TALK TO YOUR CAPTAIN
*Question*: You promised to tell us about Sue's knee; and what about Gramps, Betty and Jill?
*Answer*: Who?

     But seriously folks, I am sorry to report that Sue, Darrell and Betty will not be on our staff this year. We will miss them not only for their playing abilities but also because of the fun and spark they brought to the team.
     Sue's knee is still bothering her; in our interview she allowed as how, "If I play slow-pitch softball, then I can't do other things." Well what could I say; I'm the last one who'd recommend giving up "other things"! Sue is still undergoing physical therapy and may yet go for the surgery if we can get enough people with bad knees -- limit of two per customer -- to get the good group rate (we appear to be well on the way).
     Betty, on the other hand, already has too many "other things" going on to be available to us: specifically she has set her sights on a college degree and now goes to school 8 or 9 nights a week; best wishes Betty! Of course there is a rumor going around that, having bested her sister Mary last year (batting .083 vs Mary's .059), Betty has just chosen to coast this year!?!
     Gramps has just decided to relax this year.   In our off-the-record interview, he said, "My first year with the Mad Batters, everything was easy:   I just played as though you and Henry weren't there. But last year you guys had begun to improve to the point that about half the time you'd get a glove on the ball and deflect it so I never knew *where* it was going. This just got to be too frustrating."
     Jill is -- as we all know -- in the hospital having yucca drink drained from her knee (well it certainly has the same color).   Her doctors have essentially ruled out the possibility that a herd of gnats gnee-capped her, and they gnow tend to think she has an uncanny ability to detect gnuclear accidents at long range. Stay tuned to this gnewsletter for more developments on this one!
     Bob is also ailing fans:   shortly after I handed him his *No Shit*!?! award for last week, he doubled over in pain and hasn't been back since. Can't you take a Joke, Bob?

*Update*:
SO SUE ME:   Sue finally had the knee surgery, and she is reportedly doing fine.   Nonetheless I'm publishing this poem:
\*\*\*\*\*\*\*\*\*\*\*\*\*\*\*\*\*\*\*\*\*\*\*\*\*\*\*\*\*\*\*\*\*\*\*\*\*\*\*\*\*\*\*\*\*\*\*\*\*\*\*\*\*\*\*\*\*\*\*\*\*\*\*\*\*\*\*\*\*\*\*\*\*\*\*\*\*\*\*\*\*\*\*

# GET WELL QUICK, SUE'S KNEEDED
Here's to Sue from the gang at WAC;
We're sorry that knee surgery has you on your back.
We sincerely hope your recovery is swift,
'Cause otherwise we'll have to chip in for a gift !
And here's some medical advice from the Mad Batter's team vet:
From now on use your other leg when you pirouette !!

## LOSERS CAN BE WINNERS TOO*

Here's to the Mad Batters, whose record is pure;
    Your place in the cellar remains secure!
        Tho' the outcome was close -- it gives me shivers today --
        Your fielding stayed characteristic:
            Can you say, *"Ole"* !?!
The hitting (and missing) was full up to spec,         .
    And your speed 'round the bases got its usual respect.
        So hold your heads high and walk proud with a strut;
           You earned all the suds that you downed at Hof's Hut!

_____

*Or they can just be losers as in Going Down Aga
                        i
                          n


## THESE CLOSE CALLS ARE WEARING ME OUT

Thirty-five to twelve
    is what the record will show*,
        But how close it really was
           the world will never know.
If we'd hit fifteen more home runs
    and caught about ten more flies,
        We'd have made it past the mercy rule
           and cut them down to size.
'Cause I could see it in their faces
    as they rounded third and loped for home:
        They were really getting tired
           and weary to the bone;
Whereas our team was just getting started
    and getting the feel of the bat --
        When all of a sudden the umpire declared,
           "Game's over and that's that!"
So you see its just cruel fate
    that left egg all over our face,
        But what the hell,
           there's no other team
              as securely in last place!

_____

*Well okay, it was really 12 to 35, but that version is depressing, and besides it doesn't rhyme!

THE TUESDAY AFTER

Okay, so we lost one critical game to an arch rival – result: MAD BATTERS 8, GOING DOWN AGAIN 18.   Don't forget, they're all getting older faster than we are!?!

Absolutely brilliant pitching for a last place C-3 League team!   When you consider that Going Down Again is world renown for their patience in waiting to get the walk, our pitching staff didn't really do too bad – I know we didn't walk in 18 runs!   Attaboys Ralph and Wiley II too!   I would also like to point out that these guys don't just pitch, they are part of our C-3 class infield defense as well, moving to cover and/or backup weak spots. Ralph, for example, made a sensational tag at home plate – saving the assigned catcher (your Team Captain) from a(nother) debacle.

The rest of the defense performed damn good too, and if I had connected to Bones on a couple of easy pickoffs , and if that tall guy hadn't hit those home runs, and if there hadn't been quite as many errors, I'm sure this would have been an entirely different ballgame!?!

But however well our defense might have performed, our offense could have been even better!   Alas our hits were too few and too far between and not very far in the middle either where most of them were caught by Ollie and thrown to Leo before we got to first base.

Luckily there were essentially no fans in attendance to verify our performance in this one, my son-in-law's English isn't all that good, and I have the only copy of the video. Trust me team, when the image processing is finished we're gonna do okay!?!

Post Game Attitude Adjustment was interesting because both the Mules (our next victims) and Found On Road Dead (the following week) had K.O.ed their enemies by mercy rule; boy have we made these two teams overconfident or what!?!   I can hardly wait!   Of course Captain Kurt didn't have the faintest idea that it was us he played next, so he's probably out right now recruiting ringers like crazy.   No matter Kurt, this one is ours! And Roach, you're next!!

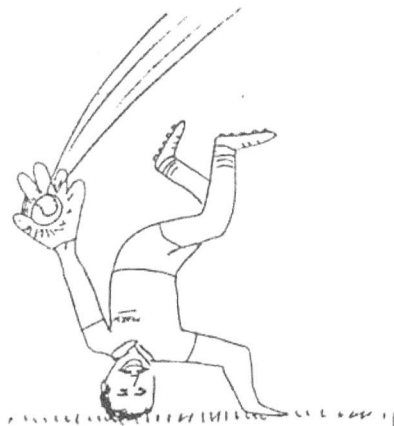

HO HUM. MARK MAKES ANOTHER CATCH.

MAD BATTER DATA FOR VIDEO UNIT
Players in nominal batting order; batting average to date and nominal defensive position listed in parens after each name. All data guaranteed to be at least somewhat truthful and accurate; no sexual harassment intended no matter how sexy the person is!

*COACH JOHN (.667, center field).* John is the team coach so any bad play executions by any Mad Batter are his fault. John is also to blame for taking over the team in its infancy during the first season (after Bones had dumped us). John proceeded to shape the team into a precision slow-pitch softball machine, and we had a perfect regular season that first year except for winning our playoff game.

*CHRIS (.500, 3rd base).* Chris is having an excellent year except she tends to stop a lot of hits to third base with her body; next year we're thinking of teaching her what the glove is for.

*BRAD (.743, shortstop).* Brad's having slightly more than a fair year: 10 HRs and 36 RBIs so far. Nonetheless his personal coach, Wiley, says there are still tricks that Brad needs to learn; since I am sworn to avoid sexual harassment, you'll have to ask Wiley yourself.

*LINDA (.429, 2nd base or rover).* Linda joined the Mad Batters after the season began, to fill in for Bob who -- as you well know -- left us unexpectedly. What a good deal that has turned out to be: not only has she played better softball than Bob ever did, but also (since she works in HR on the 4th floor of the Admin building) now we can get the passes to Disneyland without waiting for the damn elevator!

*MARK (.656, left field).* Mark has had another excellent year, although he is newly married (December), and this seems to be sapping some of his energy (surprise!). Mark's specialty is finding potholes in left field while making sensational running catches. The team vet is saving a bullet with Mark's name on it.

*RUSS (.480, right field).* Why they nicknamed him "Shuffle" is a mystery to me; Russ is so fast that if the bases were laid out in a straight line (the way they should be for C-3 League where backup is everything!) he'd have already scored a run before you could even say FO!! And that's not all.

*DAVE { BONES } (.515, first base).* Bones originated the Mad Batters for the '84 season but soon suckered John into taking over. Worse yet, Bones stayed on to "help" the team by playing first base -- just kidding, Dave!   Bones is also the team base-running coach and simultaneously serves as the Official Mad Batter Statue.

*JUDY (.125, 2nd base or rover).* For an interesting variety of reasons, Judy played with us in the pre-season games but missed the entire first half of the regular season.     And for reasons not yet clear, the team has been doing about as well now as it did before she rejoined us; if anyone can find meaning in this, I am sure it is our crack video unit?

*JERRY (.478, center & rover)*. Jerry injured himself in our last game and may not be playing tonight. It is ironic that Jerry hurt himself in the *leg* going after a flyball because everyone on the team was betting he would be injured in one of his other bodily protrusions; you have to watch Jerry's catching style to appreciate this.

*JACK DAVID (.519, third or fourth)*.   This is *The Mouth's* 2nd year as the Mad Batters' Team Captain (not to be confused with Coach; see John above). Any decent plays executed by the Mad Batters are the direct result of the Team Captain's inspirational leadership.   In some desperation, he's been played at right field lately where he has become a *triple* threat: not only can't he catch, but also he can share his thoughts (?) with both our own and the adjacent diamond.

*RALPH (.444, pitcher)*. Ralph won the Sue-Look-Alike contest (judges were blindfolded to eliminate any chance of discrimination) and became our pitcher this year. He is doing a sensational job, I don't care what they say! He has pitched every game except one, has been in trouble with almost every batter, and yet we are in next-to-last place within C-3 League. So clearly Ralph still has a lot of potential left.   And furthermore, no pitcher in all of slow-pitch softball is more cool on the mound:   penguins would shit at his feet if available to do so.   (I don't have time to fix every typo.)

*WILEY (.400, catcher, 2nd base)*. If you think you see Wiley at this game, you need to clean the lens of your camera because he is on an extended vacation helping major league baseball teams get back on track (like the *Senators*, for example). Wiley has played an absolutely sensational game this year (relative to last year) and is eyeing Bones baserunner coaching job for next year.

*JUNE (.333, catcher, 2nd base)*. June has fielded more fans (3) for one game than any other Mad Batter so far this year. She has also become a C-3 class catcher including a pre-season tag of Big Bill sliding into home and several near misses in the regular season. Furthermore her bat has been responsible for more than 75% of our hits this season (but it needs new tape on the handle, June).

*JILL (.200, catcher, 2nd base)*. Jill has improved dramatically this year. She was crippled for part of the season with knee injuries and bridal showers, but she is 100% for today's game, and we need her enthusiasm to carry us past the low points: for example when it looks like we might Mercy Rule the enemy team, she'll say something like, "I doubt it!", and so far she has always been right.

*HENRY { SHOE } (.478, 2nd base)*. Nicknamed "the late Henry" by Wiley, Henry has never been on time for a game that anyone can remember, but now that he's near the end of the batting order there's a chance he can take his turn. Henry played third base early in the season until it was discovered that Chris has a better arm among other things.

*KATHY (.000, ready reserve)*. Kathy signed on as ready reserve for the team in case we ran short of the required 2 ladies necessary for a game. So far she was called on once and played a very credible game (for the wife of our coach). Her batting average of .000 is after only 2 trips to the plate and thus by Mad Batter standards is no measure of her potential -- we sincerely hope!

The Mad Batters + Mule & the Gang

## MULE & THE GANG DATA FOR VIDEO UNIT

Names listed in random order; no telling how they'll bat or even who will show up for the game. Batting average and nominal defensive position are in parens after each name. All data is true to the best of anyone's knowledge, since this team has no written records.

*DOUG (.125, 2nd base).* Doug joined the Mules after about one-third of the season was over, when his passion for rescuing helpless animals overcame his better judgment one evening at *Chester Drawers*.

*BYRON (.125, shortstop).* Byron is the shy guy on this team, but he is beginning to respond to post game shyness therapy at *Chester Drawers*.

*{ WILD } BILL (.125, 3rd base).* When Bill was asked if he knew anything at all about softball, he said, "No, but I'm a party animal!" Kurt understood Bill to say he was "partly animal" and added him to the Mule's roster immediately.

*KATHLEEN (.478, catcher).* Kathleen is the only good ball player on this team, so with typical strategic brilliance Kurt has her playing catcher.

*KURT (.125, right field).* Kurt is captain of the Mules. He explains his role by saying, "If the shoe fits, wear it!", and then hee-haws like a jackass. It fits, Kurt!

*LOU (.125, center field).* Last year, playing 3rd base, Lou became the only player in WAC softball history to execute a triple play (ironically against the Mad Batters). Unfortunately, nobody on either team realized what had happened, and Kurt has moved Lou to center field until he stops whimpering about it.

*TERRI (.573, rover).* Two years ago Terri played for a professional women's softball team, but they missed the National Championship by one game. Totally dejected, she married Robert and is now carrying out her promise to get as far from professional-quality softball as possible.

*ROBERT (.125, left field).* Despite shock therapy (cleverly administered at work via bad designs he is asked to test), Robert still bats backwards, but at least they have convinced him to stand on the wrong side of the plate to compensate.

*KEN (.125, first base).* Ken wields a mean bat at times, but in the long run his average seems about the same as the other Mules. Ken's defensive specialties are staining his official Mule tee-shirt with sweat and trying not to look frustrated about all the bad throws to first base.

*JOE { JAYVEE } (.995, pitcher).* After helping to start this team last year, Joe suckered Kurt into being the captain; now Joe just pitches and keeps the team stats …. to himself !?!

## SNATCHING POETRY FROM THE JAWS OF DEFEAT

The last half of inning seven
    was the last chance the Mad Batters had;
        The Mules were up by four whole runs,
            but the Batters wanted this one bad.
Well, Brad's drive went right thru Bill at third,
    who saw Brad go to second and swore.
        Then Linda hit to JayVee the pitcher;
            throwing her out at first allowed Brad to score.
So now the gap was only three,
    and Russ stood ready at the plate;
        He hit a shot to Teri the rover,
            but with his speed
                the throw to first was too late.
Next Mark moved strongly up to bat,
    his reputation making him seem ten feet tall,
        And the Mules' eyes grew round
            (and several wet their garish pants)
                'cause they knew he could really pound that ball !
And pound it he did, on the very first pitch,
    but alas the wind took it foul;
        And double alas, his next long drive was caught --
            now the Mules let out their jackass howl !
Bones kept it alive with a single, however,
    advancing Russ to second base,
        And JayVee fell apart at the seams, so to speak,
            walking Judy and getting egg on his face.
Thus the bases were loaded and two were out
    as Team Captain took his strange batting stance.
        The video unit announced, "Team goat's at the plate;
            the Mad Batters haven't a chance!"
Now it's true that he was 0 for 2 on the day,
    still the odds were even he might give it a smash;
        So the air was electric as he foul-tipped strike two,
            and when the next three were balls
                you could feel lightning flash !

At the pitcher's mound JayVee was bathed in sweat,
    and the crowd's roar drowned out by his pounding heart;
        While at the plate the umpire turned his head in disgust
            as Captain expressed *his* tension with an enormous fart.
JayVee's arm swooped thru an arc and released the ball
    -- not a heart dared beat in any chest --
        And even the flies that surround every Mule
            remained motionless as the ball's trajectory reached its crest.
Down it began, picking up speed;
    watching the seams you could see it slowly turn.
        Everyone could tell that it was going to be close,
            and now every stomach began to churn.
Thru the glare off his nose
    Team Captain watched the ball descend,
        and all three muscles in his body were tense.
He knew that a Grand Slam
    was what his team needed from him now,
        preferably a clean one,
            clear over the damn fence !
And he mused on how
    he'd then be carried off on the team's shoulders
        -- as it turned out that was somewhat his fate --
For just as in his reveries
    he started a modest speech with, "It was nothing..."
        from the corner of his eye
            he saw the ball bounce on the plate!
Crawling away, the Captain was surrounded by Mules
    and hoisted up
        for a victory lap around the track.
Still standing on first,
    Judy hollered after in frustration,
        "Keep him you Asses;
            we don't want him back!"
Everywhere at beaches in Southern California
    happy people are surfing and getting a tan,
        But there's no joy among Mad Batters
            -- nor much surprise either --
                'cause their Team Captain has screwed up again!?!

**35**

## THE TUESDAY AFTER

Oops, the MAD BATTERS seem to have stepped in a road apple, so to speak, almost winning a hard fought battle with MULE & THE GANG, 11-14. Can you say, "Awshit!?!" On the other hand it was a close game all the way (C-3 League standards), and we were definitely building toward the end!

The pitching staff was never more accurate, managing to hit each Mule in the bat several times apiece.

Our defense was really almost sensational, keeping their offense pretty well in check for all but two innings. If only we'd been able to contain Jeannie's hitting I think this one would have been ours. The Polish video unit did a marvelous job of capturing John's unbelievable double play in the 6th inning – snaring Nelson's long flyball to left field and then nailing Harris going back to first base!?! Come the war I'm giving all my hand grenades to John!!

Well, if our pitching was deadly accurate and our defense was almost sensational, what can we say about our offense? Never mind they shut us out in 4 innings and held us to 2 in two other innings, look at that 7th inning rally!

Despite the drizzly, gray May weather – complete with moments of bona fide rain and low flying aircraft looking for a place to land – the throngs of loyal fans were wild with excitement over this game. Well okay, Jane left after the 4th inning, and Katie just wanted to see everything from upside down, but Lou's brother seemed amused, and the teams warming up for the next game surely knew they were watching something special. Specifically, after Chris almost got a double – unfortunately Bones was already hogging second base and Linda was camped on third – one of those warming up observed, "Well wasn't *that* special!?!"

At *Chester Drawers* for Post Game Attitude Adjustment there were *five* teams: the Mad Batters, the Mules, F.O.R.D., 5 & 5 for Fun and the Sidewinders! What a victory party!?! Well okay, *almost* everybody there was celebrating a victory. Captain Kurt had to leave surprisingly early, but Freight Train and the Roach stayed on all night is my guess. In fact many of the Mad Batters were still there when I left; good work team! Jill seemed to be making a miraculous recovery from her back problem, in direct proportion to the loudness of the music.

## TALK TO YOUR CAPTAIN
Q. You claim that the pitching, the defense and the offense all performed superlatively; so how come we *almost* won – again?

A. For a new team member, that question is a little testy, Linda, but I 'm happy to answer it anyway. I have cross-examined the team records, and the only correlation with our better performance in previous softball seasons is that Brad was younger!?!

## WHOA!   ROAD APPLES ON THE TRAIL

Here's to the Mules: each and every one an Ass,
And worse, nary *one* with even a little bit of class;
But I admit their reflexes are fast
'Cause when I buy a pitcher to replace the last
They're always the first ones there holding out an empty glass !!!

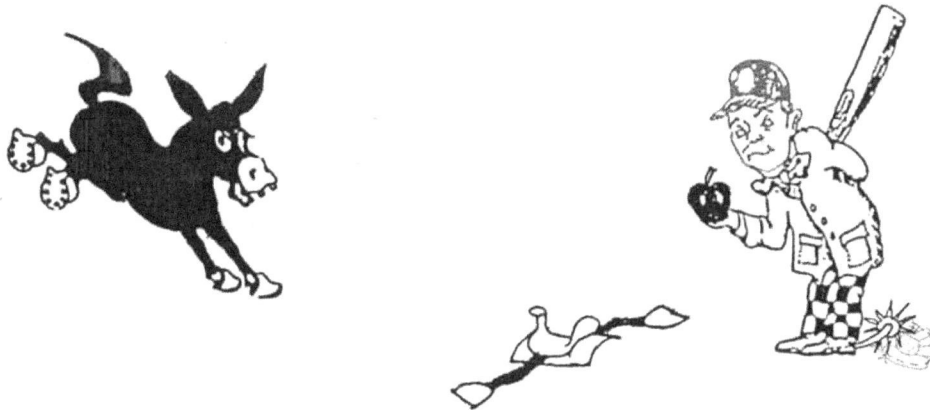

## WELCOME TO C-3 LEAGUE

Once there was a ball team called "Found On Road Dead";
By a "dain bramaged" captain called "Roach" they were led.
Their roster'd split your sides because
A funnier collection of names never was –
No wonder they Adjust Attitudes all night instead of going to bed !?!

37

THE MONDAY AFTER

Oboy, did we almost win another one or what!?! Despite intense *"I think I can"* –ing by every Mad Batter for a full five minutes prior to this game, Found On Road Dead left us at the side of the road instead, 16-4. I tend to think of this as a game where we had 'em tied at 4 – 4 after the fourth inning. Details are fuzzy after that, but somehow they got 5 runs in the 5th and 7 in the 6th – did we stay for that inning? Bones' comment: "Our losses are becoming even more convincing !"

Our pitching must have been great because almost no one walked, and their offense got 16 runs in about 50 at-bats. By perverted inductive reasoning therefore, I am hereby awarding Attaboys to the pitching staff, Ralph and Wiley II too!?!

Think of how this game might have gotten out of hand if the defense had slumped: not this time ! Everything went like clockwork – Judy showed us another incredible snare of a hot grounder – except for a couple that got past third base (guess who was on duty there this week?). Our big problem was that they kept hitting them where nobody happened to be standing, a cheap trick that is sort of a Tesdall family trademark. I guess it's the sort of thing we should have expected from a new, inexperienced team. Incidentally, Wiley I thinks I was mistaken in identifying Chris's glove as a hand puppet; he believes it is actually a pot holder.

The important thing to remember about this game is that Hiroshi blasted the Roach's very first pitch out of the park for a huge home run! Attaboy Hiroshi !!

Since this had been billed as an *ADO Historical Moment* a large mob of fans was on hand to cheer both teams. I am proud to report that despite the downward trajectory of the Mad Batters' efforts, our fans remained at our side throughout the game. Of course the better seating and free refreshments may have been a factor. Katie assured me that from her perspective (upside down) our trajectory seemed okay.

Speaking of Post Game Attitude Adjustment, your team captain almost outlasted the Mules and F.O.R.D., but 'tho I know for a fact that the Roach was unconscious, he had propped himself up between the Tesdall sisters, Diane and Dayna, and was still wearing his "I win" SEG when I gave up. Of course Freight Train was just warming up – having earlier sworn he wasn't going to stay that evening – and when I glanced back as I was leaving he seemed to be climbing onto a barrel to dance.

SOCIAL CALENDAR NOTE: Next week's game plan is to mercy-rule No Excuses in 4 innings and then adjourn to the Mancini going-away bash at Pinafini Restoranti. Never mind we will be all sweaty and dusty; the management has agreed to waive the dress code for "a select few" – but try to ditch the gloves and cleats, and no dipping your caps into the punch bowl this time!?! (Linda has reneged on her offer to let us shower at her place – negotiations broke down over the timing – but notes that her neighbor usually has his sprinklers going at about that hour.)

TALK TO YOUR CAPTAIN

Q.   You have been muttering inanely about "In-the-park home runs".   Talk is cheap – especially in your case – can you be more specific for once?!?

A.   Thank you for your diplomatically phrased question, Brad.   As a matter of fact I do have a plan for easy Mad Batter style in-the-park home runs:   Consider that the weakest spots in any C-3 League defense are the catcher, right field and second base; third base is marginal (hold your thoughts, Brad).   Thus to get an easy in-the-park home run all you have to do is get a fairly wimpy hit over the third baseperson's head.   Then you <u>just keep running</u> until you get back to home plate !   Wasn't that easy?!?   Meanwhile, the third baseperson will have dropped back to get the ball, narrowly avoiding a collision with the left fielder, rover and shortstop.   Noticing that you have rounded first and are on your way to second, the third baseperson will make a terrible throw to the second baseperson who will make a fascinating attempt to catch the ball which will thus go on out into right field. Their shortstop – always the best player on the team (now don't you feel terrible, Brad) – will watch all this with total disgust;   CAUTION: he/she may try to trip you as you go by – you know how short-tempered shortstops are !   The right field person will have no trouble picking up the overthrow from second because the ball will have rolled to a complete stop before he/she gets to it – although there will be some confusion because the center fielder, shortstop – they're quick – first and second basepersons and the pitcher will narrowly avoid colliding in the scramble.   By the time the ball is fielded you will be around third and on your way to home.   Guess what?   They will still try to throw you out at home!   So now it is you versus their catcher who will not only have you and the ball coming in hard, but also their entire defense will be converging on the plate en masse in a desperate effort to help the catcher; guess what that does to the catcher's concentration on the ball?!?   Don't even *think* about sliding; go in standing up!   In fact just stop and give the catcher a big hug !!

39

OBOY, THE FINAL '86 SEASON NEWSLETTER

Well, that was a heck of a party gang; bitter experience seems to have instilled some caution into our approach to Yucca Drinks: so as far as I know, there were no casualties! And thanks to the crashing Mules (Kurt, Joe and Bill) who gave us someone to throw in the pool (Kurt) more or less unexpectedly. Well okay, I don't think Mark was expecting it either. And it was nice to see oldtimers Lurch and the Polish Rifle again too. Thanks again to Judy for letting us into her pool / jacuzzi complex -- a great party site!

Of course everyone received an award, and they are listed herein somewhere; hopefully I will remember to accompany this newsletter delivery with delivery of your certificates too. (Thanks very much due to Joan who types the certificates, buys the trophies and generally makes the award ceremony happen -- but never shows up to be thrown in the pool by way of properly thanking her!)   Lucky for you it was too dark to read my poem, but I am including it here nonetheless. And also included are the historical stats prepared by Brad: it would appear that either we peaked last season or else we're still in the noise?

## MAD BATTERS '86, BAD ATTITUDES 0

Here's to the Mad Batters -- again -- it was another fantastic season!
You're not just another fun softball team, you're special!
... give me a minute and I'll think of a reason.
Not "special" like "Special Olympics" (although at times it's hard to tell)
But "special" like super nice people
who just don't happen to play softball very well.
Who nonetheless try their hardest to have fun in every game;
Who play every game as though it were our first,
but play to win, no matter how lame.
Whose legendary slides into first base
have never resulted in injuries requiring the team vet
('Tho in truth your best slides've been into the bench,
just in time to avoid a forfeit).
Who retire to Post Game Attitude Adjustment to celebrate
-- no matter we win, lose or draw --
And who do so with such decorum and class
that even the Mules are in awe!
Who adjust their attitudes so enthusiastically
before they stroll out *Chester Drawers'* door,
that most of Friday morning is spent in the head
reading the newsletter to learn what happened the day before.
So here's to the Mad Batters:   it's been 3 seasons;
Time really does fly when you're having a good time!
Thank you all very much !!
(And yes, I know it seems like hours now
your Team Captain's been reading this stupid rhyme !)

40

## MAD ABOUT THIS CHRISTMAS PARTY

Christmas Cheers to the MAD group
    (even the ones with a funny sounding name):
        Without your global insights
            our proposals just wouldn't be the same.
On the other hand, now that I think about it,
    I'm not sure exactly what MADness you really do,
        Although I know it's global and that
            our proposals just wouldn't be the same without you!
I'm really glad to be here
    and to share your eats and drinks
        -- I'm sure your insights are global
            no matter what everyone else thinks!
But never mind the details
    'cause this party is really classy.
        (I just wish Bob's secret bean dip recipe
            hadn't made me get so gassy.)
Of course we'll eat and drink and sing
    and have a really merry time,
        And then we'll suffer in silent misery
            while we read this stupid rhyme.
And we'll keep our hands to ourselves
    lest we be charged with sexual harassment
        (Although they're having a lot more fun
            at the SOBAD party where the perverts went.)
We're glad to be together
    at this special time of year;
        Our teamwork and our friendships
            are what make life seem so dear.
We'd like to think our work's been good
    and made the Nation's enemies a lot more cautious.
        So Merry Christmas and Happy New Year
            (I've got to stop now --
                this poem's starting to make me nauseous!)

DARN! ONLY 12 MONTHS THIS YEAR!
Here's to the calendar persons of Technical Pubs:
 Who currect r speling and fix r flubs;
  Beneath whose blue pencils all our writing must pass,
   and who've many a time saved our poor illiterate A.S.S.;
    'Cause it's not the content -- all that technical bullshit --
     It's how many pictures and how eloquently you say it!


A CLASS ACT, NO MATTER WHAT HAND HE'S DEALT
Here's to Jim:
 twenty-five years in WAC's zoo,
  And before that at arch rival BAC
   he also put in a few.
So he's seen lots of aerospace programs
 -- the list must seem endless --
  And after SOBAD you'd think he'd know better
   than to gamble on A.S.S

But Ashly suckered him again:
 "FPA' s are (probably) no sweat !"
  And Stan wasn't here to help him
   assess the (long) odds on that bet.
Well now that there are problems
 and competition is growing strong,
  It's time to look back and wonder:
   in twenty-five years of service,
    where did Jim go wrong?!?


PROPOSAL PRAYER
Dear God, this proposal bless,
 And thank you for our leader Wes;
  But God, why now?
  And how, Lord, how?
Holy shit, God: what a mess !!

RED TEAM BLUES

Monday I was assigned to a Red Team
     and given one of our proposals to review.
          I finished the job just last night,
               and now I'm feeling blue!
First I read the customer's requirements;
     then I read what we'd proposed.
          You guessed it: there was scant correlation!
               ... an entire pad of Deficiencies I composed!!
It wasn't even clear to me
     that I had read the right proposal,
          And I wasn't sure whether to just laugh at the Joke
               or take it straight to the garbage disposal.
The themes tended to be shallow and asinine,
     like "We have the right design!" and "It's the best!"
          And the technical stuff was truly amazing:
               "Our design weighs 200 pounds but is small enough
                    to be carried in the soldier's vest!"
Another among my "favorite" lines
     was where "Heisenberg was uncertain, but we're not!"
          And "Now that our entire staff is upgrading the test set,
               our detector's sensitivity has improved quite a lot."
The good news is: there were plenty of graphics,
     'tho what they meant was a mystery to me.
          Half of them were packed with unlabeled data,
               and the other half too small to see.
I read the proposal carefully,
     and I tried not to judge too quick,
          But by the time I had finished the Introduction & Summary
               I was already unbelievably sick.
I continued reading into the System Description
     -- now I wish I had been more cautious --
          'cause when I finished Section 2.1
               my mouth was dry and I was feeling nauseous.
Even so I proceeded forward
     -- relatively speaking I liked 2.2 a whole bunch --
          Alas, Section 2.3 was one step too far:
               I ran to the head and barfed my lunch!
Well needless to say, I used up many red pens;
     when I was thru the sight wasn't pretty!
          But I managed to sum it up
               in a single Principle Comment: "This proposal is totally shitty!"

## SAMPLES PER DWELL

The question is: How many to use?
      One, One-and-ahalf or Two are the views.
            Tho' Nyquist said Two, he's long since been dead;
                  So we started afresh--let's try One someone said.

The next thing we knew, heavy flak was pouring in;
      Awshit! We'd committed a Federal sin.
            Please forgive us; we're sorry and humble as hell;
                Would you believe we were joking?
                Two sounds just swell!

## A YEAR'S END MUSE

Here's to Allen from the Engineering Improvement gang
      We started our group with a terrific bang
            To search for a way to help Systems flow
                And enhance the rate at which our programs grow.
Unfortunately we sank -- up to our A.S.S.'s --
      Into Guidelines and Directives and group consensus's;
            And each meeting's start was painfully slow,
                Albeit much faster than our progress would go.
So here's to Allen and our fourth free lunch!
      We're really grateful: thanks a bunch.
            I wish we could reciprocate
                And a full set of solutions clearly state.
But alas, the puzzle's far from clear .......
      ... Perhaps next lunch let's have some beer?!?

## ALAS POOR YORK; I KNEW HIM WELL

Here's to the Rescuees:
    We're glad to have you aboard.
            We're sorry that your program sank --
                    albeit corporate profits have soared!
So don't think of yourselves as failures
    'cause your personal loss has become the company's gain,
            And we'll be glad to take over your building
                    'cause this one leaks when it begins to rain …
Of course there'll be some adjustments:
    You'll be a "C-maggot" or "A.S.S.hole" instead of a "Big Gun",
            And you'll have to adapt to schizophrenic air conditioning
                    In a building where you never see the sun;
But other than that it's wonderful
    And there's certainly work aplenty,
            And you can begin to relax and not worry about hiding
                    From the cameras of 20/20 !?!

Some of my poems dealt with more profound issues than others …..

NO SHIT

How many person-hours are wasted in the head
    When they could be spent enhancing
        our product's performance instead?

Of course I realize that we all generate
    a certain amount of bodily waste,
        And I'm not suggesting we fool with Mother Nature
            and attempt these functions with undue-haste.

Indeed, at *that* end of our head call
    the problem doesn't exist;
        Nay, instead -- and believe me
            this really has me pissed! --

It's after you've heeded nature's call
    that needless time begins to burn,
        While you struggle with
            what ought to be the simplest aerospace problem:
                making the roll of toilet paper turn !!

VERSE 2: A CLASS ACT

Here's to the head of facilities
    (I hope you don't think this too crass)
        Thanks for resolving the toilet paper problem:
            A shitty job but handled with class !!

## CHAPTER 4. THE '87 SEASON

### THE TUESDAY AFTER

Gone but not forgotten, last Thursday the Mad Batters almost humbled another A-League class team, Hit & Run !   Even though the final score (about 25-10) seems to favor H&R, and even though they got thru their batting order twice for every once in our case, the rate of progress was clearly beginning to favor the Mad Batters in the closing innings!

Wiley II too's pitching was entirely credible: I never saw him give them anything really decent to hit, so whatever runs they managed were probably just lucky swings.

Speaking of lucky swings, we must note your team captain's first-ever* home run!?! (Where were that bat, strong breeze & gravity anomaly when I really needed them at the end of last season?!? )   Bones deflated my moment of glory with this conversation:
Captain:   "You missed a great game, Bones!   You'll never guess who hit a home run?!?"
Bones:   "Jill ??"
Captain:   "No, it was me !?!"
Bones:   "You're right; I never would have guessed."
*And, as it turns out, "only-ever"

Our defense was impenetrable for the most part (read, "Team Captain only handled the ball twice" – Hiroshi backed me up like a shadow).   Of course Brad was everywhere again, involved in more than half our plays.   Two of Brad's famous *Incredibly Careful Throws* resulted in tags at homeplate, the most dramatic of which came when Hiroshi chased down a would-be home run, throwing to Brad who then pegged it to Ralph for the tag at home!   Having taught Brad everything he knows about the game, the Wiley I was beaming like a proud father.

### TALK TO YOUR CAPTAIN

Q.   Last week – for the second time – you foo-pawed what's-her-name, Dayna's last name, and you also called Michel "Michels".   Earlier in the pre-season it took you a week to learn that they were Raascholes with a "c".   Melanie has yet to show up at a game because you initially spelled it "Melany", and Mark even quit the team because you called his wife "Alexandria" instead of Alexandra!   In short, you have a totally careless attitude about people's names.   With such inept intrapersonal skills, how can you expect to captain a major C-3 League team?
A. Who wants to know?

### TALK TO YOUR CAPTAIN ... REPRISE

Q. How many questions and answers were in last week's TTYC?
A.   Three and two, respectively; so if the last answer didn't strike you as having had a question, then maybe you should look again.   There, I'm sure that's all cleared up now!?!

## IT'S ONLY A(NOTHER) GAME

Ugly rumors notwithstanding,
    the players of Haagen-Dazs
        (With a couple of notable exceptions)
            apparently don't wear bras.
On the other hand, it seems to me
    those suckers can really bat
        And kept our crack defensive unit
            chasing this hit and that.
So despite outstanding efforts,
    we seem to have lost again;
        Tho' after innings one and two
            I thought we might actually win!
A bunch of the Mad Batters
    hit real or near home runs,
        And June got hits and an RBI
            -- no kidding! Bless her buns!
Mark's pitching blazed, and of
    his plate coverage no one could scoff;
        Laura really hustled,
            and u-no-who yelled his A.S.S. off.
So we were definitely on our game
    and played exceptionally great;
        It's just that winning this one
            was not to be our fate.
But what the hell, we're six and oh*;
    Way to go Team!
        Let's keep up this momentum
            and this incredible head of steam!
If we can roll on thru the playoffs
    and make it thru this year,
        We'll have spent more time than anyone
            crying in our beer!

---

*Well okay, it's really 0 and 6, but that version is depressing, and besides it doesn't rhyme!

## ON BEING 8-0 IN C2 LEAGUE*

Going Down Aga
                    i
                        n
                            didn't,
        and instead Mad Batters did.
            I think our basic problem
                    was a ringer, name of Sid.
From where I watched,
        his hitting and his catching were not nice,
                And it didn't really help a lot
                        that we only got thru the batting order twice.
And I personally made some errors
        -- with my shoes on I lost count after ten --
                And had some help in that particular stat
                        from some others now and then.
So we let a big one squeak by us,
        and now we're eight and oh*;
                I don't mind so much the losing
                        as the taste of eating crow!
But the Loggers also lost this week
        -- a few of them today are mental wrecks --
                And next week we get the challenge
                        of going full steam after S. E. X.! !
So gird your loins and psyche
        and forget this last week's pall,
                'Cause as Bones noted at Post Game Attitude Adjustment:
                        "You just can't win ' em all"      !

---

*Well okay, it's really 0 and 8, but that version is depressing, and besides it doesn't rhyme!

## IS IT TOO LATE TO MAKE OUR MOVE?

Well we lost another close one
　　　-- how can I say this without being lewd --
　　　　　Instead of getting S. E. X.
　　　　　　　the Mad Batters just got screwed!
(There, I think I managed;
　　　with that version the censors can be bucked;
　　　　　Or at any rate it's cleaner
　　　　　　　than the version that rhymed with "lucked" .)
Although it would have been better
　　　if we'd pulled ahead and won,
　　　　　As you might have *a priori* guessed
　　　　　　　playing with S. E. X. was terrific fun!!
So now its on to the playoffs:
　　　we're the only team the Hot Dogs beat.
　　　　　Although it'll spoil our perfect record,
　　　　　　　let's roast the Hot Dogs in defeat!!!


## AWSHIT, WE WON ONE

No wonder Post Game Attitude Adjustment
　　　took quite a bit longer than usual last night:
　　　　　The Mad Batters roasted the Hot Dogs --
　　　　　　　we can't seem to do anything right!
Our offense and our defense
　　　actually played exceptionally well
　　　　　And blew our otherwise perfect record
　　　　　　　completely all to hell !
So now we're tied at 9 and 1*
　　　-- screams of anguish I have to muffle --
　　　　　But just you wait until next year
　　　　　　　when we show 'em the Mad Batter Shuffle !

*Well okay, it's really 1 and 9, but that version is depressing, and besides it doesn't rhyme!

50

## THE MONDAY AFTER

Well wasn't that special!?! Except for another bad data point (8 runs) in the second inning we woulda' had 'em! However the official score was ETA PIZZA PI 13, MAD BATTERS 9 after 7 long innings of struggle. At the half-way point of the season, guess which team is in last place gang? Anyway it was another fun game on the path to nowhere in particular.

Continuing long standing tradition, I would like to start by reassuring the pitching staff that nobody else wants their thankless task, and thus they both win gratefully offered Attaboys by default. Oh sure, we saw some walks, but there was a strikeout (Ralph this week) and several nice hittable pitches too. Remember, if the pitching staff didn't put just the right amount of body English (Sue where are you?!?) on those things they'd all be homeruns instead of doubles and triples.

Our offense was pretty well summarized by Judy's dash from the toilets to the plate where – presumably a little pooped – she grounded out on the first pitch and reportedly observed, "What a shitty offense!" Special mention must go to the offensiveness of Linda and the Wiley I who played/batted/ran despite leg injuries. (The team vet was a little disappointed, however, since he had just cleaned his pistol before the game.)

Ironically the defensive story is also summarized by Judy's absolutely brilliant running, diving stab – okay, would you believe standing-still with arm outstretched, head turned & eyes closed? – stab of a line drive to end the 4th inning! Attagirl Judy!?! The rest of the defense also performed impressively – for example after Bones somehow snared a line drive he almost got another unassisted DP this week, but before he could say, "Feet don't fail me now!" the Pi's star lady ballplayer was back to the bag. I really have no idea how so many runs could have gotten by us. Well okay, I remember one run going by as I tidied up around home plate, but that was a fluke.

Sideline activity verged on chaos. Chris & Bart brought this monster animal of some kind who variously dragged Ralph's kids and/or the backstop around in pursuit of one of our softballs – hereafter known as "the slimy one" – while Katie busied herself demonstrating that personal energy goes in inverse proportion to some power of the age-mass product. As a direct consequence I'm pretty sure the Pi's 8-run inning was the result of a severely distracted umpire!?!

Post Game Attitude Adjustment was a fantastic almost-victory party since the Mules and F.O.R.D. had joined us in "close games". To my delight, Freight Train had to leave early, and after the Mule's late shift (Jane & Jeannie) left, soul survivors Captain Kurt and your Team Captain dug in and prepared to outlast F.O.R.D. .... It soon became clear, however, that Roach and the Tesdall sisters were actually getting their second wind – Steve was just breaking wind, but it did give him more room on the dance floor. After an in-depth discussion of what perverse power the age-mass product should be raised to (Karen's guess: "You're both shitheads !") we gave up and left.

.

IT'S BEEN FUN TO KNOW YOU
Here's to the Ford Pickups:
    'tho their attendance has been
        a whole lot less than 100 percent
            their hitting has been a helluva lot better
                -- homeruns so long no one knows where they went!
On defense of course they're somewhat less graceful:
    they can't catch grounders or flies nor throw,
        But what the heck, that's only an indication
            that they've lots of potential to grow!


YOU'RE OKAY IF I'M UPWIND
Here's to Mule & the Gang:
    a herd of jackasses and proud of it too! ?!
        And before every game (to establish their "rep")
            they all stomp their feet in donkey "doo",
And then for good measure
    -- its disgusting but true --
        they rub some in their hair;
            Well needless to say there's no mistaking this team
                for they have an unmistakable air!
As if their style of softball wasn't enough!
    'cause they play like a bunch of asses,
        And would have scored nary a single run
            had not opposing defenses fled upwind
                while their baserunner passes !!

## THE TUESDAY AFTER

The thing to remember about this game is that despite being outnumbered – eight great Mad Batters versus a whole herd of Asses – we led 'em 2-0 going into the bottom of the first inning!   After that we kind of relaxed in a couple of innings and ended up letting the MULES gallop over us 14 – 7.   We'll see you in the playoffs Kurt !

The regular pitching staff (Ralph) handled the entire game and did his usual almost great job.   Since we didn't have a 3rd baseperson or rover, Ralph put lots of spin on the ball to ensure the Mules would hit it toward the right side of our defense … Unfortunately this was often the wrong side of our defense too.

Not counting the rodent carried off by a hawk as we all watched in amazement (Kurt's comment: "That was one of the people we played last week!"), Linda was the only injury in this game.   She forgot the Team Captain's advice about sliding into first base and instead ran head first into the Mule's first baseperson.   As she laid there contemplating the extent of her neck injury, the most painful part was having to listen to the bad jokes.   Team Captain: "Since you don't seem able to move, why don't you just take over coaching here at first base?"   Wiley's counter-offer:  "Why don't you just _be_ first base?"   Nice try anyway Linda!?!   (Medical bulletin:   Linda reports that it only hurts when she parallel parks).

## TALK TO YOUR CAPTAIN
Q. Is there any excuse for dropping a perfectly catchable flyball?
A. Yes, Alan, there are actually quite a few.   My personal favorites are "Gravity Anomaly" and "Temporary Amnesia" – which in fact was responsible for the one I missed last week: I had forgotten that Brad has learned to back-up every defensive shot I get, and it startled me to see him rushing into my territory!

## MAD BATTERS '87, BAD ATTITUDES 0

Well wasn't *that* a special season:
    An entire string of games we almost won !
      With total offense only 106 points
        But an unmeasurable amount of fun !!

In accordance with tradition established by John
    We've faithfully kept all the stats –
      For example, John's four season average .633
      Based on a total 113 at-bats.

Thus the accompanying tables of data reveal
    A history of good and bad news,
      But what may not be entirely clear from this
        Is that Mad Batters could never really "lose";

'Cause every Mad Batter is definitely a winner,
    Even the ones who can only barely hit;
      So what if our defense tends to deflect rather than catch
        And so what if our throwing is usually for shit!?!

The stats, you see, don't cover important stuff:
    Like the fun we had during and after each game
      And how super are the people who comprise this team –
      So what if their teamwork was usually lame.

Well okay, it's been enormously enjoyable,
    And I'm sorry to see this season halt.
      Although we almost won every game,
        It's 'cause Contra hearings were so distracting –
         i.e. it was all Ollie's fault!?!

## SOUND EFFECTS

In the earliest days of electronic voice technology the available "vocabulary" was extremely limited, and -- at Dori's request -- I managed to generate the following ditty within those limits.

HIGH -- THIS IS DIGITALKER
READY TWO GO
FOUR A GREAT TIME
TRY ONE DOLLAR
IN THE SPACE BELOW
FOUR A GREATER TIME
PLUS S-E-X
TRY A MILLION DOLLARS --
PLEASE NO CHECKS !?!


## I CHOSE THE WRONG CURTAIN AND I GOT ZONKED

Here's to Dori Ann ("Zonk"):
the best office-mate for which anyone could yearn
-- Or at least that's what I told Frank Smith
when I convinced him that now it was *his* turn.

Sharing an office with Dori is like boxing ....
with your hands tied, taking hit after hit;
And like the boxing analogy the best part
is at the end when you finally quit !

Dori's a complex and fascinating person;
she's not nearly as weird as she seems;
It's just that she never lets on that she's normal
except during the night in her dreams.

So it's really been different and interesting
-- like riding in a barrel over the Falls --
But now it's time for a new game called,
"avoid getting Zonked in the halls" !!

## HEY, LIGHTEN UP; IT'S NOT HAPPENING TO ME

Here's to Don and Betty Trailar
     and a marriage of an incredible sort:
          Incredibly fun, incredibly romantic,
               And -- given divorce statistics -- probably incredibly short.
And speaking of short, Don, here's some honeymoon advice:
     Don't rush sticking your Trailar "tongue"
          into Betty's Trailar "hitch";
               First warm up her motor and lubricate all the parts
                  or you may learn the meaning
                     of the cliche "Life's a bitch !"
Meanwhile, Betty, be patient and understanding;
     Don's nice, but he's not too bright;
          His head's still full of all that macho shit;
               you'll have to use cunning to train him right.
And both be aware that marital bliss is accompanied by problems,
     like sharing the bathroom
          and arguing over every decision you make.
               You'll both have to make sacrifices and surrender half your freedom
                  ... Are you sure marriage isn't a big mistake?
Well never mind now; go forward you lovebirds;
     share the good times and the bad times come what may.
          I'm really sincerely glad you're getting married
               because I never liked either of you anyway!
But seriously folks, I'm happy for Don and Betty
     and think they're really first rate.
          May your union last forever and your dreams all be fulfilled;
          May good health and happiness be your fate !!

------

And I was never invited to give another wedding toast ever again !??!

## WHAT'S A NICE KID LIKE YOU...?

Congratulations to Bob and Valerie,
    and Happy Birthday to Francis Shelby !
        The miracle of birth is now behind
            -- and speaking of history --
                your carefree days might as well be!
Because now the contest really begins:
    parenting's a mixture of pleasure and pain,
        and it's not going to be easy for daughter Shelby either
            what with you two being so hard to train.
But lucky for baby, her crying's tuned to the frequency
    that makes Mom and Dad's life a living hell;
        So within a couple of months
            you'll be giving her not only what she needs
                but everything she *wants* as well.
Good news: at that point it begins to be fun;
    watching a child learn and develop's a joy to be seen;
        And it's important to stock up on all these wonderful memories
            -- you'll need to fall back on them when she becomes a teen!
Meanwhile we're all very happy for you three
    and for all the love that you share for each other
        ... But don't get carried away (albeit none of our business)
            unless you want Shelby to have a baby sister or brother!?!

## A SHORT POEM FOR YOUR BIRTHDAY

Here's to Joan:
    the short secretary we all adore.
        (Uses file drawers one, two and three
            as steps for climbing to file drawer four).
A very Happy Birthday Joan;
    Tho' we can all see that you're short,
        If measured in units of Lady-per-Inch,
            you're slam-dunk champ of the court!!

## ANOTHER JOAN POEM

Here's to our favorite short lady named Joan.
    Spends her days typing and answering the phone.
        May your birthday be the best
        And the same for all the rest
We'd still like you even if another foot you'd grown !!

## SHORT NOTICE
Here's a poem that's really short:
    HAPPY BIRTHDAY SPORT !

    or

Many people are born in the fall,
    And many people are slender and tall,
        And many people are grouchy and mean
        With a face and disposition too ugly to be seen!
Happy Birthday Joan: you're not like any of those people at all !!!

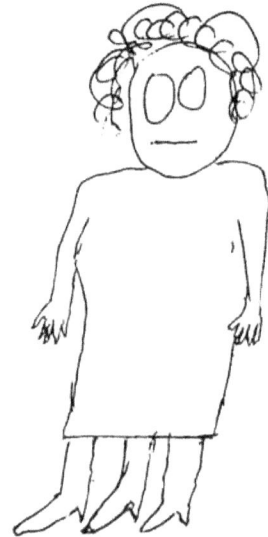

## HEY, IT'S ONLY A JOB WELL DONE

Happy Secretary's Day Joan:
    we all think you're absolutely the best!
        And we not only think so on this one short day
            but also on all the rest.
We thank you for all that you do for us all
    -- especially the donuts and the typing so swift --
        And by way of demonstrating that our feelings for you are sincere,
            we all chipped in on this gift.
It cost us the better part of ten dollars,
    and the salesperson said it was quality stuff,
        But no matter how extravagant we went for the present
            we can never ever thank you enough.
Well that about says it; we hope you got the message:
    we think you're a lady of the most incredible sort:
        Incredibly fun, incredibly smart, incredibly nice
            -- and incredibly short !!

## SHORT REFRAIN

Re Secretary Days:
    Skip the praise;
        Where's the raise?'.?

## SHE WENT THATAWAY

Here's to Lori: she's heading out the door
    Toward a well deserved retirement
        from Wonderful Aerospace's paper war.
She's been buried in a lot of bullshit
    but always came out smelling like a rose!
        We all wish her the best for the future,
          down whichever path she goes.

## TAKE A NUMBER

Here's to Rosanna and Brad:
    two beautiful people and both first class;
        Congratulations on August 20, 1988
          as into wedded bliss you pass!
I'm really happy for the two of you,
    and I know you'll really do great;
        But try to control the size of your family:
          my boat's capacity is only about eight.

## PERIODIC POETRY

Periodically Patricia stayed abed,
    during which periods she really saw red!
        Her friends wanted so
        to help stem the flow
That one even suggested using
    a loaf of Wonder Bread!?!

## PAUL'S POEM

Here's to Paul McKristen who's headed thru the door.
>He's turning out to pasture and won't be back no more,
>>So I thought I'd write this poem in honor
>>>Of his life that's come before.

Paul's been around a lot of years and designed a <u>lot</u> of shit:
>CRAY and FPAD and the F-18 Servo and an ugly box called DIT,
>>… but the pre- and post-formatter
>>>Are the ones he tries hardest to forget!

He's an archaic example of a gentleman and a scholar;
>Of guys his age there's no one who stands taller
>>… and his 3-coin luck's so bad
>>>That his average cup of coffee costs a dollar! *

Tho' Paul will soon be gone his memory will linger --
>Or at least the smell of his cigar (geezus what a stinker !) –
>>… and his personality: so warm
>>>That he actually <u>wore out</u> his middle finger !?!

So here's to Paul – and I mean this not in jest –
>Your work's been great, and you've certainly earned this rest.
>>It's been enormous fun to know you,
>>>And we wish you all the best !!!

---

*Recall this was written in the '80s.

## THE DARTS JUST BOUNCE OFF

Here's to Dan McCorski – one helluva funny name –
>But without it on our org charts, WAC just will not be the same !
>>We'll miss his "What-me-worry?" grin
>>No matter how deep the shit he's in,
And most of all we'll miss the fun
>Of assigning *him* all the blame !?!

## ODE TO ELI

There once was a wise man
     named Elias Heizman:
          Experimental physicist and roof repairman extraordinaire!
Whose tests in the field
     Produced both fun and data yield,
          And whose lasers transmitted naked ladies thru the air!!

From smokestack to smokestack
     His merry band pressed their attack
          to measure pollutants released to the sky,
And ever the trail blazer
     Eli developed our first $CO_2$ laser
          and aligned it -- according to legend -- by necktie!

A true gentleman and scholar
     -- though at times known to holler --
          there're few careers as remarkable as Eli's.
As outstanding in scientific and human worth
     As he is in personal girth,
          His absence will leave a vacuum of enormous size!!!

## OFF THE MARK

There once was a wild Polish Rifle
     Whose wife -- name of Ann -- was an eyeful !
          When asked to reply
          How he liked working with Eli,
A loud scream he was forced to stifle !!

SAY "PHYSICIST"--(Gesundheit !)

Here's to our leader, Dr. Paul,
    from the Design Engineering mob:
        We'd like to express our regard for you;
           We think you're doing a helluva good job !
And we're all behind you all the way
    (including Willard, Fred, John and Joan)
        -- Except for negotiations with Ralph or Eli:
           for those you're on your own.
Looking back on your career in physics,
    we see an incredible amount of broken glass,
        and millions of small holes burned with ruby lasers
           are now enlarged by lasers filled with gas.
But looking back over your career in management here
    is a remarkable case of "*Deja Vu*":
        Didn't John and I meet two decades ago
           in this same office with a much younger you?
And needless to say, in walking to work all those years
    I'm sure you've noticed quite a change.
        Whereas it used to be easy to cross a small two-lane road,
           now it's a major highway with 500 lanes!
(Well okay, I took poetic license with that last little rhyme;
    Paul understands that sort of thing can have its use;
        In fact in some of *his* poems
           the application of poetic license
              clearly verges on poetic abuse!)
Oops! Again my little ditty has gotten out of hand
    so I'd better cut it short;
        Here's a toast to Dr. Paul:
           you're a gentleman and a scholar,
              and a person of the nicest sort!!

## CHAPTER 5. THE '88 SEASON

ONE MORE TIME ...

As the countdown to the end of this '88 season closes rapidly on Zero, the MAD BATTERS have begun to get their act together, fielding a full 10 person team (eventually) to deliver a stunning 26 – 4 victory to POULTRY IN MOTION – but guess which team had the 4?  The feathers are still flying after this broiling hot game!?!

   At the mound again Ralph used every pitch in his cookbook to hold Hank's paltry flock of poultry to a mere 26 runs in 3.5 blazing innings.  Ralph's pitching was significantly enhanced by Chris at third base who devastated the random Poultry batter with an occasional terrorized shriek, "HERE COMES THE COLONEL !!"

   Aside from the pitching and verbal abuse, however, our defense mainly depended on John to catch flying Poultry balls to get us out of each inning.  Hank definitely had the green light on, and the Mad Batters had a workout chasing hits – not to mention the agony of our one-arm scorekeeper, June, trying to keep track of it all.

   Alas, Hank's victory dance was dampened considerably in the last inning when he broke his leg sliding into home plate – why anyone in C-3 League would slide into any base other than First remains a complete mystery to your Team Captain.  The team vet was fairly drooling at the prospect of performing surgery on a Poultry and had a little pop-up thermometer all set, but the darn Paramedics elbowed him aside.


   NICE SLIDE, HANK....?


Hey Hank, the Mad Batters penned for you this very sweet little poem;
    We're all real sorry that you broke your leg sliding into home.
        And of course we hope your recovery is swift,
            .... 'Cause otherwise we might feel compelled
                to chip in for a gift !?!
    And here's some really good medical advice
        Straight to you from the Mad Batters' team vet:
            From now on use your other leg
                whenever you pirouette !!*

---

*Of course* I know this has been used before!   Plagiarism is the sincerest form of flattery??????

## CHAPTER 6. THE '89 SEASON

ONE MORE TIME AGAIN …

Well, there's another slow pitch softball season ('89) behind us, and the MAD BATTERS went out in fine style, almost winning a big one from VK CHAPS 13 – 9. In a game almost full of highlights, here are a few:

The pitching staff performed almost flawlessly, predictably peaking in this last game of course. Ralph got a little blatant with the sandpaper in this game, but he thought there were major league scouts watching.

The defense performed almost brilliantly, determined to cover up for errors at first base. (Just kidding Bones !) Chris's hand-puppet/pot-holder glove missed a hit to 3$^{rd}$ base in the 3$^{rd}$ inning and instead the ball just hit her in the pot, so to speak; ouch! Bones made an almost unbelievable (*) diving, groveling catch of the ground ball to first base that finally ended the game. Attaboy Bones; a great season.
(*) Unless you remember that Bones is an expert break-dancer too.

But perhaps I digress … meanwhile back at the game, every Mad Batter got to first base at least once this time. In fact , June and the Wiley I got to first, second and/or third about 3 times each within one minute of classic C-3 League suspense and action! With one away in the 4$^{th}$ inning, June was on first and Wiley was on second when the Team Captain drilled this enormous pop-up to the VK shortstop. Since our crack staff of base coaches had clearly warned both runners to tag up if it was a flyball, June & Wiley both came back to their bags the minute the ball was hit and then proceeded at their usual blazing speed toward 2$^{nd}$ & 3$^{rd}$, respectively. Unfortunately "tag up" means "after the ball is caught" and not "after the ball is hit" – these subtle distinctions are really inappropriate for C-3 League – so now June & Wiley had become fair game! Well what with all the base coaching and confusion among even the VK Chaps, our two almost-fastest base runners proceeded to dash back and forth between bases 1, 2 and 3 like ducks in a shooting gallery. When the dust finally cleared, VK had logged 6 outs: 1 fly out, 2 throws to the bag and 3 tags on the baseline. The umpire had to call a 15 minute timeout to regain his composure. Almost Attagirl & - boy anyway June & Wiley; it's the thought that counts.

Post Game Attitude Adjustment at Chester Drawers Inn was understandably wild and woolly. F.O.R.D. had beaten the Mules, and Sidewinders had secured C-3 League's First Place by beating the Field Rats. Notwithstanding ballgame results, the Roach and I decided there should be a really meaningful playoff at Chester Drawers, for *"Life, the Universe and Everything"* as the Roach put it.

ANCIENT HISTORY
Wonderful people are born in January
    when the weather is really cold.
        (Or at least that was true many years ago
            -- this birthday group's really old!)
Their combined age is CLXIII years,
    an average of LIV -- That's Amazing !
        We're talking at least a four alarm fire
            if the forest ranger spots all their candles blazing!
So treat them nice:   not just because they're old
    and losing all of their hair,
        But rather because -- if your luck holds out too --
            you'll need a friend who's familiar with Medicare.


HAPPY BIRTHDAY LADY !!!
This poem's a little late,
    and your birthday is now just history;
        And since I want to remain your friend,
            Herein your new age remains a mystery!
I hope you enjoyed your special day
    And reflected on all the time that's passed away
        And plan to enjoy to the fullest your remaining years
            -- of which there's now one less to be!


HEY, YOU COULD PASS FOR 38 ANY DAY
Here's to Mary (belated) for Birthday 39:
    Please relax and enjoy it;
        we think you're doing fine !
Of course you *are* another year older,
    and time does take its toll;
        And teenage children only accelerate the clock
            as toward old age we roll.
But what the heck, you're looking great,
    and at second base there's none more sporty.
        So don't give your age another thought
            -- at least until next year when you're forty !!

WEATHER GOEST?
23 years ago a 24 year-old boy from the farm
        Said, "I studied meteorolgy; I'm gonna go live where it's warm!"
            So he packed up his suitcase
            And went to work at Wonderful Aerospace;
now 'stead of a rooster, he wakes with clock radio alarm.

So here's to my good friend John on birthday 47:
        He's adapting to Southern California
                -- at first he thought he'd died and gone to heaven --
                He's becoming laid back and cool,
                    Spends his weekends tanning by the pool
And stays up late to catch Dr. George weather at eleven!


ANOTHER GOOD DEED GONE WRONG
Larry's fifty, and he's never looked better!
        (Oops! that's both the good news and bad;
            my face couldn't be redder!)
                A half century plus nine months ago
                His mother passed up a chance to say, "NO !"
And now we're stuck with the world's oldest bed wetter !!


HAPPY BIRTHDAY BARBARA (HOW OLD?)
Remember when you were a young girl
        and dreamed of being a movie star?
            And you wished that you were rich enough
                to drive your very own car?
And you couldn't wait to develop
        and become glamorous and more mature?
            And the dream of being married to an older man
                for you held more allure?
Well on this Happy Birthday, Barbara,
        you can look back on your youth and laugh;
            And reflect on how many of your dreams came true
                ... in your case, I'd say about half !

## STILL ON FIRE

Holy smoke, Bill, it's your birthday:
        you've made it to another!
                Albeit a cliffhanger for awhile there
                        -- you've had more ups and downs
                                than your balloon-driving brother!
So you've certainly earned your cake this year,
        and we hope you really enjoy it,
                And we're all very happy
                        with your recovery from the stroke
                                (you still speak more clearly then Wit !!)*

_____
* Wit was a really wonderful colleague from Poland.


## AUGUST BODIES

Birthday people of August are usually incredibly hot!
        -- Which is not to say on the other hand
                that incredibly cool they are not --
They come in all shapes and sizes,
        Are generally full of fun and surprises,
                And in fact are five of the people
                        that we all admire a lot !!


## UNBELIEVABLE FOR HIS AGE

Birthday greetings to my friend Jerry:
        still a nice guy
                even 'tho he's one year older.
His parents' frolicking one winter
        produced this huge, red-faced baby
                in the fall when the weather turned bolder.
                        Jerry builds our FLIRs -- we're up to about number 10 --
                        And repairs them again and again and again,
And is so strong he can carry
        6000 pound nitrogen bottles,
                one on each shoulder !!

## HAPPY BIRTHDAY TO MS. X

Here's a birthday poem to Ms. X:
    I promise not to tell how old you are today!
        Besides, you look so incredibly young
            that nobody would believe me anyway.
You're classically beautiful, your hair is a crown,
    you dress in clothes that are elegant but bright:
        They suggest rather than cover a body that's stunning,
            whose vision keeps men awake all night.
Yet there's more than just beauty: you're a fascinating person as well
    with a mind that's quick and witty and smart.
        You're nobody's bimbo nor coldly liberated either;
            you're a mixture of logic, intuition and heart.
I'm delighted to be your friend; you're thoughtful and fun,
    and naturally I'm in love and in lust with you too.
        But of course every other man feels the same way toward you as I
            -- and of course you already knew.
So don't get alarmed that I put it in writing
    (perhaps I should have been more cautious);
        I only did it to wish you a Very Happy Birthday
            -- I hope this poem doesn't make you nauseous!


    or


## HOT DAMN !!

Here's to ladies over forty
    from a man who's somewhat older:
        You're not only more beautiful than ever,
      but you're wiser
          and a helluva lot bolder!

YUPPIE BLUES
Once there was a yuppie who grew older every day.
    Not just linearly but *exponentially* her time sped away.
        When she turned 32
        She was feeling so blue
That she filled her entire Jacuzzi with Oil of Ole.


HAPPY BIRTHDAY PUMPKIN HEADS
What kind of kid is born in the month of October?!?
    The month of Halloween -- the thought leaves you sober! --

The month of goblins, ghouls and witches ...
    of course, there's probably no connection;
        So what the heck, let's not think about it;
            let's just relax and enjoy June's confection.

… On the other hand, there were more birthdays this month
    than any other: a total of eight;
        And if there *is* a correlation with Halloween,
            what do you suppose will be our fate?

Do you suppose there'll be more gremlins in our work,
    and project costs and schedules will more often double?
        Oh well, most of these people are too old now
            to give us much more trouble!


MERRY BIRTHDAY
Here's to the birthday people of December:
    Johnson, Daley, Ryder-Smith and Shoe;
        You have not only our best birthday wishes
            but all of our sympathies too.
'Cause we know that you've never received full respect
    what with combining your birthday and Christmas together,
        Not to mention the fact that your parent's frolicking in the spring
            led to your birth in the most shitty of weather.
So we hope you enjoy this wonderful celebration,
    (and that June's carrot cake doesn't make you get farty).
        Happy Birthday to you four! -- and oh, by the way,
            this is also the Department Christmas party.

**70**

## CHAPTER 7.  THE SEVENTH SEASON

OBOY IT'S THE '90 SLOWPITCH SOFTBALL SEASON

Sensational practice game team!   I'm sure we demolished 'em … after certain score adjustments are made to account for the fact that there were more Mules than Mad Batters. (Unfortunately, looking at our HUGE roster nobody's gonna believe that.)   Anyway I can tell it will be a(nother) helluva season. New pitcher Hurricane Jim almost showed great promise: Attaboy!?! Defensively it was pretty much Eric to Bones, but the rest of the infield (Alan & Kathy) almost did a fine job too.   And of course what can we say about our outfield, Bob P, Laura and Team Captain, this week?   Well okay, we could say that Team Captain needs a lot more practice, but I meant what could we say that was nice?   Yeah, I couldn't think of anything either.

Offensively it was another story, however!   The way I have decided to keep score this year is:
> (a) I count the number of Mad Batters at the game (can range from 8 to 19 on any given night
>   – tending toward the 8 apparently).   Let's call this number X (remember algebra?).
> (b) I count the number of times Laura bats; call it Y.
> (c) Since I know she made the last out in each inning, I figure there were two other outs
>   before that; call it 2.
> (d) I count the number of Mad Batters still standing around on a base without a glove on (not
>   always a sure sign that we're still on offense, but usually a reasonable clue); call it Z.
> (e) Everybody else must have either hit a homerun or stolen home from first base, so the total
>   score has got to be:
$$Score = Y \times (X - 3) - Z$$
For example, this past week there were 8 Mad Batters and Laura batted half-dozen or so times, and I can't ever remember any Mad Batter standing around without a glove on, so our score was pretty obviously about 46.347.   A similar, albeit more circular, calculation leads me to conclude that the Mule's piece of the score pie was only 3.14159, which is why I stated that we must have won this one in the first place!?!

TALK TO YOUR CAPTAIN
Q. If I screw up and don't quite hit a homerun, and now I'm standing all embarrassed on one of the bases, shall I take a big lead off after each pitch or should I stick close to the bag until I'm sure it's a hit?
A. Well of course this dilemma won't come up much for Mad Batters, but since you've asked, it's like this:   Rule 4b states that you may lead off as soon as the ball leaves the pitcher's hand (don't fudge; umpires love to catch you leading off too early!), and – given that catchers in C-3 League never have any arm – there is almost no chance of being picked off; therefore a big lead off is a wonderful thing to do!   But beware, if the Mad Batter hits a flyball, only run half way to the next base because if the flyball is caught you must tag up at your original base before proceeding.   Personally, when in the outfield (on defense that is) your Team Captain likes to *drop* such a flyball just to see the confusion it causes for all the base runners.   With practice this can turn into an easy triple play !!!

## HOT DAMN WE ALMOST WON A BIG ONE

Even tho' the Mad Batter offense peaked early in this game, the defense held tight in almost every inning to almost give us a stunning upset victory over the LINE DRIVERS … but alas not quite!?!

Sensational defense by Hurricane Jim who not only pitched his usual fantastic game but also seemed to be involved in every play – he pitched a lot of pop-ups! – and repeated his famous break-dance-before-throwing-to-1$^{st}$-from-his-knees trick; this really rattles the enemy offense !

Jim Hurl covered left field like a blanket.   I will never forget the *Where'd this come from??!* look on Hurricane Jim's face when, having moved from the mound to cover home, all of a sudden there was the ball, which Jim Hurl had hurled from deep left.

Miscellaneous memories: Marcia stabbed a mean line drive to stop the Line Driver offense in one inning.   Alan learned the meaninglessness of the Team Captain's promise to back him up in right-center field!   Bones executed another feet-don't-fail-me-now race to the bag after scooping up a ground ball near first base, beating the unfortunate Line Driver (who was limping as I recall) by well over a microsecond!

## TALK TO YOUR CAPTAIN

Q. I notice that – despite the detailed records you insist on keeping and your computerized game plans – last week you erroneously reported that BobC scored the game-winning run and that Eric slid into third, whereas actually Eric not only slid into <u>second</u> but also it was Eric, not BobC, who made the game-winning run.   And this week we were beaten by the Line Drivers whose only paperwork this entire season is gonna be their darn Waivers!   So what's the point of all this Mad Batter paperwork????

A.   Geez, Judy, it's only a scoresheet!   … and would you please press harder on the pencil; these are a little tough to read.

Team Captain backs up another play!

## FANTASTIC FINAL GAME TEAM

Well, with the last bugs in the Mad Batters' Computer Optimized Strategy & Tactics (COMPOST) game planning software having been tracked down and corrected, we finally got it together: In a hotly contested fun game both our Stealth Offense and our Stealth Defense worked to perfection, giving us a convincing 7 – 18 loss to F.O.R.D. and earning us not only 3rd Place in C-3 League and 33rd of 36 overall, but also -- as BobC put it so delicately -- *"Total mediocrity in the lowest league*!?!" Congratulations team, a brilliant end to our '90 season!!!

## SO MANY PITCHES, SO LITTLE TIME

Here's to the Mad Batters of 1990: a really fantastic team!
    Whose 1990 preseason potential fulfilled my wildest (softball) dream!
        Alas a few runs slipped past the defense,
        All our Grand Slams failed to reach the fence,
But what the heck, we're 33rd out of 36 …
        …not as mediocre as it may seem!???!

MOVING POETRY
Once upon a time there was a damsel in distress:
    Requested moving muscle to help change her address
        And I sincerely wanted to help this friend
          to relieve her of some stress.
Alas, her plan conflicted with an earlier one of mine
    To take other friends sailing out o'er the salty brine,
        And of course, the lady smiled bravely and said,
          "That's okay; everything will be fine."
With dock lines in hand on the appointed day at dawn,
    After a restless night I stifled a yawn;
        A moment's guilt -- then we were gone.
The sea was calm; the air was clear;
    The horizons were far -- but my conscience was near,
        And the crew was puzzled that I drank so much beer.
We moored at Catalina; we swam; we ate;
    We rowed and hiked and played until the hour was late,
        ... And as I fell asleep I wondered about the lady's fate?
I envisioned this giant desk -- her arms and legs sticking out beneath it --
    All the way down at the bottom of the stairs where they had lit,
        And heard her very frustrated voice saying, "*Awshit!*"
Next day my mood was better, and I was feeling a lot more glib.
    After all, "This boat's for escape!", I thought to myself as I hoisted the jib,
        And besides, think what a helluva nice letter
          I'm going to receive from Women's Lib!!


CREW BLUE
Here's to the crew: they're almost always late!
    The appointed hour comes and goes,
        but I'm still waiting at the gate.
Tho' I invited twenty -- hoping somehow to maybe see ten --
    Only two showed up ...
        ... *Surprise, Surprise*: the skipper's frustrated again!
But I've grown philosophical:
    Tho' a skipper's life can be maddening and hard,
        Sitting at the dock waiting for crew
          sure as hell beats working in the yard!!

SHIPSHAPE !!!

To the vessel *Laurie D*
 and to her skipper and namesake / crew:
  The skipper of the *Dave-y-Joan's* sends his greetings;
   it's a pleasure sharing a slip with you.
Making it into my slip without hitting your boat
 is my priority navigational goal,
  But please be advised that whenever Laurie's on deck
   my vessel's essentially out of control.
Her beauty's so gorgeous and stunning
 that every crewman becomes a fool,
  And if -- oh please! -- she's wearing a bikini
   my deck's disgustingly awash with drool.
With tongues hanging down and eyes bugging out
 crew rushes starboard to better take stock
  And 9 times out of 10 even *I* get distracted
   and wind up hitting the dock.
So next time you see us coming into port
 please lock her in the vault,
  'Cause any property damage and/or broken hearts
   are otherwise all Laurie's fault!

THEY MADE IT AGAIN !!
Here's to the crew of Flight 891:
    the service was great and the flight was fun!
        Only one passenger got horribly sick this time,
            and he hadn't even tasted the food
                nor stopped to read this rhyme.
(Thank heavens they'd booked lots of doctors before leaving,
    and the stews had stocked up on barf bags for heaving).
        But other than that the flight was great,
            and the food was palatable (I cleaned up my plate),
The air was smooth all the way to Hollywood,
    and -- as everyone knows --
        any flight you walk away from was good!!


FLIGHT 708
Here's to the crew of Flight 708:
    The ride was smooth and the service was great!
        I'm always impressed with Republic's style;
            They see that the passengers enjoy every mile.
It's the way every airline flight should be done:
    Not sober or grim;
        if you make it, it was fun!


STEPPED IN WHAT?

Dennis Smith went hunting for deer
    Or bear or whatever else came near.
        All he got was the flu
        And a sprained ankle too ...
Of Rambo Smith animals have *nada* to fear !!

JUNE IS BUSTING OUT ALL OVER

Here's to June who bakes the cakes;
　　Who wires our boards neatly
　　　　even when their diagrams are a ball of snakes;
　　　　　　And who patiently rewires them
　　　　　　　　after we discover our mistakes.
Here's to June who always looks pretty;
　　Who cheers us up with her smile
　　　　even when her day has been shitty;
　　　　　　And who even now is smiling
　　　　　　　　while she's forced to read this stupid ditty.
So here's to June: it's your birthday; relax and take a breather!
　　May the coming year be fun and happy;
　　　　of pain and sorrow may you have neither.
　　　　　　We love your cakes -- and by the way,
　　　　　　　　Rick told me to add that your buns ain't so bad either !!


　　BE THERE !?!
A New Year's party is in the air;
　　At June and Buddy's amazing
　　　poolside estate is where!
　　　　Of course there'll be music and dancing
　　　　　-- bring your favorite record to play --
　　　　　　And bring your favorite dish of food to share
　　　　　　　at a fantastic midnight buffet.
Soft drinks, beer and coffee
　　will be available for all to see,
　　　But if you require something harder
　　　　then of course please BYOB;
　　　　　And we trust good taste and decorum will (as usual) be the rule;
　　　　　　Or to put it more directly:
　　　　　　　NO PUSHING OR PEEING IN THE POOL !!

**77**

# The
# MAD BATTERS

Dave Gryvnak
John Chudy
Steve Tidwell
Art Telkamp
Mark Lewandowski
June Orr
Dave Calvert
Ralph Bailey
Judy (Abraham) Harwell
Wiley Bird
Darrell Burch
Brad Layman
Mark Martella
Bob Brown
Betty Roberts
Chris (Sadony) Bainbridge
Henry Shu
Jill (Suarez) Sullivan
Russ Walker
Sue May
Jerry Hoffman
Kathy Chudy
Joan Wragg
Linda Scholl
Wiley Bird Jr.
Rick Costa
George Hayne

Hiroshi Kadogawa
Melanie LaShell
Judi Munday
Phillipa Matthews
Lynn Narasaki
Marcia Cohee
Dennis Finn
Bob Prodan
Alan Snodgrass
Kathy Snodgrass
Suzy Boyd
Bob Chandler
Debbie Ellwood
Jim Hann
Darcy Hann
John Moore
John Dennison
Karen Dennison
Eric Manton
Patty Manton
Laura (Waltzer) O'Sullivan
Judy (Zink) Calvert
Jim Hynes
Lore Hynes
Jeff Groussman
Dave Michika (video)
Grant (Scruffy) Carlson (video)

# GOT XMAS ?

MAD OR MERRY: WHAT'S THE DIFFERENCE?

Merry Christmas from your team captain;
 here's wishing you and your family and friends
  My very best for your well being:
   may the coming year be filled with bliss that never ends!
May all of your wildest dreams come true;
 may the obstacles to your success move aside so you can pass;
  And may your automobiles need nary a single repair,
   nor tires nor oil nor gas.
But if misfortune should somehow befall you
 -- like getting locked overnight
  with your millions of dollars in the family vault --
   Please remember that I'm the one
    who wished you only good things;
     All the bad shit is somebody else's fault !!

# Xmas Poems Past

**December 1967**

Dear Family and Friends

Although a particularly memorable year this was not,
  we nonetheless enjoyed it a heck of a lot.

With Janet and Robert our life was quite busy;
  in fact, more precisely, it was kept in a tizzy.

Robert's quite curious -- he tastes every toy;
  Janet asks questions and tries every ploy.

Irma has kittens: the count's up to ten
  … Oh, by the way, Joan's expecting again.

During the daytime Joan does lots of housework,
  and Dave does the yard work, his homework and work work.

Tours of L.A. with some friends, and Las Vegas,
  were vacation this year -- the bills they still plague us.

But we surely had fun and hope *you'll* visit us here;
  Meanwhile, MERRY CHRISTMAS and a HAPPY NEW YEAR !

DAVE, JOAN, JANET & ROBERT

P.S.
Now this poetry's through (bet your head is sore);
  I took it in school -- don't you wish I'd learned more!?!

**December 1982**

Dear Family and Friends,

Again this year we're running late,
    that always seems to be our fate.
        So much to do, so little time,
            and now we're stuck with this damn rhyme !

We can't recall a year so fast,
    but what the heck, it's been a blast !
        An early low -- boat on the rocks --
            is now behind -- we learn from our knocks.

Repaired like new, we've sailed here and there,
    seen harbors and dolphins; with friends we share.
        Our love for the sea is still number one;
            Six years of building did not spoil the fun !

Janet's high school graduation really swirled;
    Farewell old friends, hello new world !
        Robert and Julie work toward *their* turn;
            He drives now -- Yikes !! -- she makes boys yearn.

Dave's mom and dad had a Fiftieth bash
    attended by all, and the gift was cash
        to pay for Hawaii -- a trip by air,
            although we had offered to sail them there.

Dave's brothers and Joan's we have all seen this year
    and their families too; the memories are dear.
        So our lives have been busy, our health has been great,
            and we wish you the same -- you're really first rate.

This poem's now done, the page is full
    Merry Christmas, Happy New Year -- have a nice Yule !!

**81**

**December 1984**

CHRISTMAS 1984

Here's wishing Christmas Cheers to all our relatives and friends
and a Happy New Year to you all as well, as the old year ends.
The five of us are well and good, and life is still going strong,
and (hopefully) Janet's bridegroom Andrzej
will be joining us here before long.

She married him in Poland at a village called Szczawnica.
(Since you can't pronounce it either I can rhyme it with whatever-ica !)
Now Janet's back here waiting -- her patience is on a short tether --
while two government bureaucracies try to get their acts together.

Robert is a senior, but his goals are still uncertain.
(We hope he doesn't choose to marry behind the Iron Curtain!?!)
Julie's now a junior and a really excellent scholar
and sings in the Edison High School choir
and at football games she can holler !

In May we went to 'Frisco for a very fun mini-vacation
and for Denny's wedding to Linda -- it was a really nice occasion !
The rest of the summer was fast and hot: a heat wave was our fate,
and I lost track of the weekends in Catalina,
but I remember they were all great !

Now fall is here, and the days are getting quite a bit cooler and shorter,
so I suppose its time to stay at home and do the chores I ought'er
and to write you all this Christmas poem to say you're not forgotten
and to say we think a lot of you
-- tho' our correspondence habits are rotten !?!

So Seasons Greetings and Merry Christmas as I close this little rhyme;
Here's wishing you the Happiest of New Years,
and may it be your best of all time !!!

**December 1985**

HOLIDAY HEADLINES and Season's Greetings

Merry Christmas from the Calverts and Happy New Year too !
    We hope this finds you all feeling fine
        and that good fortune has followed you.
Our year has been busy and happy:
    Janet's husband Andrzej arrived June 24
        and joined her in their Costa Mesa apartment
            ( 'twas another 2 weeks 'ere they opened the door !)
Son Robert graduated from high school in June;
    his mind and body continue to grow taller.
        Julie's high school experience continues;
            She's a hardworking excellent scholar !
Joan & Dave spent a week in Washington D.C.
    ( it was so beautiful it made Joan weep ),
        and we spent a small fortune on Janet & Andrzej's reception
            but gained memories that we'll always keep.
Dave's dad had surgery on the arteries in his neck;
    The surgery went fine with no hitches.
        Brothers Woody and Jerry came here too for morale;
            We kept the whole hospital in stitches !
Now this rhyme's at an end ( yes I know you're relieved)
    and it's time to post it ( late again ) in the mail.
        Our sincerest best wishes for your future well being;
            Our thoughts are with you wherever we sail !

**December 1986**

MERRY CHRISTMAS

Well '86 has come and gone;
    for the most part it was a blast !
        Nonetheless we're not going to count this year ( either )
            because it went by way too fast.

Youngest child ( ? ) Julie
    -- with long blond hair and tears flowing --
        became a high school graduate in the spring
            And enrolled in the fall at UC Santa Barbara
                where she continues to study and row and sing.

Robert now works two jobs -- that's amazing --
    as well as being an OCC student;
        While Janet and Andrzej continue to build their nest egg:
            working hard, being frugal and prudent.

On the hottest day of the summer we crossed the desert to Phoenix
    (a 2.3 liter Mustang's no match for the heat);
        Dave's Class Reunion was great though
            -- despite a lot of old people --
                and it was cooler when we made our retreat.

Then business and pleasure took Dave & Joan to the Northwest
    in the middle of the month of July;
        We whirlwind-toured Seattle and Expo in Vancouver
            and marveled how late the sun stayed in the sky.

And of course it's been our pleasure to do a lot of boating
    around the harbor and to Catalina offshore;
        It's especially nice to share these voyages with friends;
        We only regret we can't do it more.

Perhaps '87 will have more weekends than 52
    .... I wonder who made such a dumb rule?
        Meanwhile have a Merry Christmas and as well a Happy New Year;
        Our best wishes are for you & yours this Yule !

## December 1987, '88, '89, '90, '99, '01, '04, '07 & '15 ...

*Created in 1987, this became my fallback Xmas poem*
*when all else (frequently) failed:*

Merry Christmas and Happy New Year;
    here's wishing you and your family and friends
        My very best for your well being:
            may the coming year be filled with bliss that never ends!
May all of your wildest dreams come true;
    may the obstacles to your success move aside so you can pass;
        And may your automobiles need nary a single repair,
        nor tires nor oil nor gas.
But if misfortune should somehow befall you
    -- like getting locked overnight
        with your millions of dollars in the family vault --
        Please remember that I'm the one
            who wished you only good things;
                All the bad stuff is somebody else's fault !!
Merry Christmas from our family to yours:
    Wishing you all health & happiness in the New Year!

## December 1992

Here's to all our wonderful friends:
    We sincerely wish you the best.
        Our '92 days and nights have been busy
            -- we really need a rest !

Married in Avalon the 20th of March,
    we honeymooned in Bora Bora.
        Was it fantastic, you ask, all that tropical splendor?
            What can I say: give me more-a more-a !!!

Other than that -- thanks to the 'quakes --
    we now live a little more north;
        So from Laguna Niquel and Judy and Dave
            Merry Christmas, Happy New Year and so forth !

**December 1997**

Merry Christmas from Judy & Dave in Florida
    and Happy New Year too !!
        We hope this finds you well and happy
           … and the stock market didn't make you blue?

We love our new home at Burnt Store Marina
    -- we're 10 miles from the nearest stop light !
        The people are great, the weather's fantastic,
           and mosquito-spray DC-3's are a sight !

Of hurricane threats there was nary a one
    -- ironically California ducked two !?! --
        but we did have three 'gators ( 'tho rather small )
           which were relocated to some lucky zoo.

We thoroughly enjoyed all 38 visitors
    -- *The Tour* has become really nice.
        The highlight ( of course ) is boating thru Charlotte Harbor,
           and we only ran aground once or thrice.

Tho' 10 miles by 30, the harbor averages 10 feet deep
    so a skipper is wise to be cautious ….
        …. Merry Christmas again. I've got to stop now:
           this poem's starting to make me nauseous !

**December 2000**

Fotos only

Merry Christmas from our Family to Yours:
    Wishing you all health & happiness in the New Year !

**P.S.** If you don't like the way we count our votes in Florida,
    you can just get on I-95 and drive back to one of the other 56 states !!

**December 2002**

Merry Christmas & Happy New Year

Top Ten Reasons We're Moving Back to California

10.  Our "kids" lied: you DON'T have to move to Florida when you retire !

9.  Does the phrase "Up to your ass in alligators" ring a bell?

8.  Boats at the back door, warm tropical waters, thousands of harbors: where's the challenge!?!

7.  My GPS got full.

6.  Sanibel lighthouse: navigation warning or mid-channel marker?

5.  Clean, clear air smells funny !

4.  Fred moved to Florida.

3.  Not paying any State income taxes in Florida just seems wrong!

2.  One word: Shopping.

1.  We want to be more like Raymond's parents!

Merry Christmas from our Family to Yours:
Wishing you all health & happiness in the New Year !

## December 2003

Merry Christmas from our family to yours:
>Wishing you all health & happiness in the New Year !

No more 'gators
>No more snakes
>>No more frogs leaping,
>>>for heaven sakes !
No more hurricanes blowin'
>No rain pouring down
>>No sharp cracks-o-thunder
>>>turning my underwear brown !
No boats at the dock …
>( No endless boat chores ! )
>>"Charter" = less work,
>>>more boating to yon shores
Now earthquakes we get
>And huge wildfires too,
>>And Recall Elections
>>>-- can you say, Governator who!?!"
Did I mention the traffic?
>Twenty-two lanes at the Y !
>>During rush hour crawl
>>>there's time to count them while you cry.
But it feels like we're home now,
>Where our journey ends,
>>With old friends and family …
>>>… tho' we do miss Florida friends!
So Merry Christmas and Happy New Year;
>On earth, Peace and Goodwill
>>…. Okay, I've got to stop now;
>>>this ditty's starting to make me ill !!!

## December 2005

It's December already, and I'm running out of time.
    So my standards will be even lower
        for this year's little rhyme.

Christmas came upon us so swift it was amazing.
    I wish it was still summer
        with sunshine all ablazing.

Instead the temp is dropping -- I may need a big snow blower !?!
    ( Like I said: this year poetry standards
        are significantly lower. )

It's going to be a cold one -- yesterday one of the golfers wore a sweater ! --
    and there are other signs
        it's gonna get worse before it gets any better.

Icicle lights are drooping from the Spanish red tile roofs
    ( it's a wonder they don't break
        under all the reindeers' hoofs. )

And on my walk to Starbucks it was plain for all to see
    that it had snowed on one of the neighbor's lawn
        in the outline of a Christmas tree !?!

But what the heck, we're mostly indoors and happy as can be
    with AOL and Photoshop
        all running on Windows XP.

Did I mention I was rushing this poem, and I've still got stamps to stick?
    Merry Christmas and Happy New Year !!!
        ( I hope it didn't make you sick. )

Merry Christmas from our family to yours:
    Wishing you all Health & Happiness in the New Year !

**December 2006**

The Christmas Season is now upon us; 2006 is racing to an end.
 It's time to stop and count our blessings,
  thinking of family and every friend.

( This year's poem was started early, providing time for eloquence and class.
 Not like last year's which was rushed and hurried
  and was mostly just pulled from my ass. )

We cruised up the Rhine at a leisurely pace ( you could barely hear the wake's hiss )
 ending up in Lucerne to relax and unwind
  and eat chocolates as made by the Swiss.

Of course we don't normally indulge like that: I mostly eat twigs and dirt,
 and I exercise almost daily it seems
  unless something comes up or I hurt.

Janet and Mickey enjoy a cabin in Big Bear, Leo thinks WVA is terrific,
 Robert turned 40, Terry does Mud Runs,
  and Julie sailed across the Pacific.

If our social life seemed reclusive this year -- some may have thought me dead --
 it's only because I was overwhelmed
  with projects such as *The Bed*:

Started in early spring, made of wood, 'twas delivered in early winter,
 and "sleeps" pretty good, according to our friend,
  except for an occasional splinter.

Did I mention the "Master Suite" remodel?   This project is still underway;
 A whole new look will be completed and done
  before Santa comes Christmas Day.

Meanwhile Best Wishes from San Clemente
 ( not far from the San Onofre nuke );
  May 2007 be your best year ever !
   … and may this poetry not make you puke !?!

Merry Christmas from our family to yours:
 Wishing you all Health & Happiness in the New Year !

## December 2008

Again this year I'm running late
     ( … which sums up my entire '08 ! )
          So much to do, so little time,
              And now I'm stumped by this darn rhyme!

Hence this holiday you'll get off easy:
     My poem's too short
          To make you queasy !?!


## December 2009

Why can't I ever seem to remember
     To start this rhyme before early December?!?
          … Causing sleepless nights and lots of stress
              And excessive use of my margarita blender !

On the other hand -- tho' it's oddly perverse --
     I cherish the time it takes to write this verse,
          Reflecting on family and friends ( here and gone )
              With fond memories that warm my universe.

Was that last line poetic license abuse?
     Was a reference to the universe too obtuse?
          Hey: get over it, it'll probably just get worse;
              For example, my candidate never shot a moose !

But I digress; 'tis time to be of good cheer,
     This merry holiday time of year
          When our very best wishes go out to you:
              All our family and friends, both far and near.

## December 2010

A decade into century twenty-one
  It's fair to ask, "Are we still having fun?"
   The answer of course ambiguous:
   'Tho the year's been fairly big for us
It's already December but this poem's just begun !?!

Fortunately the fotos that surround
  Tell our yearlong story without a sound
   And yet to many eyes they scream,
   "Hey look: check out that awesome scene !"
….. Or at least, "Hey look: Dave's gained another pound !"


Merry Christmas from our family to yours:
  Wishing you all Health & Happiness in the New Year !

**December 2011**


I started writing in January this year
  To "*en-poem*" deep thoughts I'd remember,
   But I dove so deep that when I awoke
    -- Oh damn! -- It was early December!?!

Nevertheless, there's plenty of time
  To pen something truly and utterly profound;
   And here it comes now …
    …. No wait, that was gas;
     What a rude and disgusting sound!

Two-thousand-eleven was a wonderful year:
  We joined Judy's cousin for a cruise down the Rhone,
   … And a couple of months later we adopted a dog … !??!
   Now we can hardly leave *Gizmo* alone !

He's totally sweet, he barks almost never,
  We love watching him at play or at rest …
   … Plus we're reluctant to let him out of sight indoors
    'cause his "toilet" habits are uncertain at best.

But I'm sure we'll outsmart him -- 'tho *when* is unclear --
  And he'll stop chewing on everything pretty …
   Then someday in the future we'll get a full night's sleep …

OMG:  HE JUST ATE HALF THIS DITTY!!!

## December 2012

In 2012, the Mayan Calendar said,
      by December 21 we'd all be dead.
            So: to start this poem or procrastinate?
            The latter of course,
                  .... and now it's too late;
Thus you'll just have to suffer all these fotos instead !?!


\*\*\*\*\*\*\*\*\*\*\*\*\*\*\*\*\*\*\*\*\*\*\*\*\*


## December 2013... !?!

The first draft of this poem was deemed *Bizarre!!* by those who edit;
      It was suggested I retrieve each copy, take it to the garage and shred it !
            "But *The Voices in my head* ...," I pleaded
                -- real sincere and with obvious piety --
                  ... Met with icy stares and veiled invitations
                    to join the Dead Poets Society.

So now I'm back at square number one,
      and I've missed my poetic deadline.
            There's a very good chance I'll have to work late,
                staying up way past my bedtime. ...
... ( Or not ? ) ... '13 was yet another amazing year gone by;
            Tho' with some lows, overall our year was mostly high:
                Enjoying family and friends we love, plus some travel too,
                As shown in all these fotos
                    -- Our very best wishes to ~~most~~ *all* of you !!!

## December 2014

*Even after prolonged reviews (starting in November) of previous poems, by the second week of December I still had ZERO inspiration for the 2014 ditty, so I'd almost resigned myself to replaying the "All the bad shit..." version.   Then, given the MAJOR computer struggles I'd undergone in 2014, I realized that plagiarizing from my 2005 Xmas poem was perfect !?!*


It's December already, and I'm running out of time,
        So I'm plagiarizing extensively for this year's little rhyme.
                Christmas came upon us so swift it was amazing.
                        I wish it were still summer with sunshine all ablazing.
It's going to be a cold one -- yesterday one of the golfers wore a sweater –
        And there are other signs it's gonna get worse
                Before it gets any better.
But what the heck, we're mostly indoors and happy as can be
        With AOL and Photoshop all running on ~~Windows XP~~
                                ~~Windows 8.1~~
                                        Windows 7

Did I mention I was rushing this poem,
        And I've still got stamps to stick?
                Merry Christmas and Happy New Year !!!
                ( I hope it didn't make you sick. )


*P.S. Tho' I ignored several of Judy's correct-English suggestions ( on the grounds of Poetic License ), I caved in and changed "I wish it <u>was</u> still summer" to "I wish it <u>were</u> still summer".     I'm still not convinced !?!*

## December 2017

Why can't I ever seem to remember
    To start this rhyme before early December?!?
        … Causing sleepless nights and lots of stress
            and excessive use of my margarita blender !

On the other hand – tho' it's oddly perverse –
    I cherish the time to write this verse,
        Reflecting on family and friends (here and gone)
            with fond memories that warm my universe.

Judy's star, more than a year in the sky,
    shines brightly as ever in memory's eye.
        She'd be pleased how I accomplish our domestic chores
            … except caring for houseplants, which tend to die.

But I digress: 'tis time to be of good cheer,
    this merry holiday time of year
        When my very best wishes go out to you:
            All our family and friends, both far and near.

    Merry Christmas from our family to yours.
    Wishing you all Health and Happiness
    in the New Year !!

## December 2018

Just family fotos, mostly at restaurants
                    (Carmin's comment was, "*Looks like you're well fed!?!*" )
and this note at bottom:

**There may not be a poem here, but overall Dave had a very nice year!?!**

**December 2019**

The holiday season is fast upon us
  So Dave's composing a Christmas rhyme,
    Expressing in poem his fond regard for you all:
      Every neighbor, friend, family member of mine.

Alas, until the last minute he waited
  So as usual this poem's pretty rough.
    For example he matched words "*rhyme*" and "*mine*"
      And tho' noted he thought, "*Close enough!?!*"

But moving on I'll close with this:
  I think you are truly first rate.
    May your Christmas be merry and 2020 the best;
      May good health and happiness be your fate!?!

Merry Christmas from our family to yours.
 Wishing you all Peace and Happiness in the New Year !!

# Got 80 ???

### ANCIENT HISTORY, Part 1

Here's to all my family and friends:
Having *you* in my life means a lot to me.
I've ridden this planet 80 trips 'round the sun
(How many more are to come is life's mystery).

Thanks to you, I've enjoyed almost every day,
So I wish *you* all happiness, come what may.
Please enjoy to the fullest your remaining years
– of which there's now one less to be.

# T + 4,560,000,080 and Counting

80 trips around the sun
is all that Dave has got.
To many people younger than me
That seems like an awful lot !?!
But in perspective,
before Dave's 80
Earth had almost 5 **Billion** to show,
And while Dave's got maybe 5, 10 or 20,
Earth's got another 5 **Billion** revs to go !!!!

### ANCIENT HISTORY, Part 2

Wonderful people are born in January
when the weather is really cold.
(Or at least that was true many years ago
-- this birthday boy's really old!)
His age is LXXX (four score) years –
That's ancient and truly Amazing !
We're talking at least a four alarm fire
if the fire marshal spots all his candles blazing!
So treat him nice: not just because he's old
and losing all of his hair,
But rather because -- if your luck holds out too --
you'll need a friend familiar with Medicare.

ENJOYING IRRELEVANCE    or    NOT QUITE DEAD YET

I am truly ancient;
      since Judy died I live alone,
          But my "children" live nearby
               so now and then I see them
                    or now and then we talk on the phone.

My stepson and his family
      are a nearby source of joy as well,
          As is his older brother living in West Virginia
               and apparently doing swell.

Along with everybody else
      this virus has me trapped indoors,
          So I take more naps than usual,
             but while I lay here
               my brain really roars.

I'm remembering all the things from my past --
      at my age that's a huge amount –
          And I've stored many questions and points of view …
             … that nobody seems to want.

Of course I know that's how life goes,
      when I was younger I didn't give a shit,
          and only pretended to be listening
             while my elders babbled on
               like they'd never quit!?!

So now I just stand on the sidelines,
      watching problems gain ground
          like a herd of *elephants*,
             But at least I've managed to write a rhyme
               making light of my new *irrelevance*!??!

**100**

GOT MILK?
Medical scientists are generally assholes;
      for job security making up mysterious Latin words,
          But their latest research is so amazing
              that I'm giving high praise to those incredible nerds!?!
They've sorta discovered the way aging works,
      and maybe a path to longer life,
          But as usual their explanation is so complex
              that you've thought to slit the speaker's throat with a knife.
I'll try to explain in everyday English
      using words that you learned in first grade,
          and tho' a bit long, the lesson's not painful;
              Just pay attention, don't be afraid.
At the molecular level males and females are the same,*
      our bodies are made of billions of cooties.
          (*Except that the males like jokes about farts --
              what your mother quaintly called "*tooties*").
A cootie, you see, is like a little sausage,
      a strand of *fusilli* attached like a horse's mane …
          (Pasta makers are also assholes: when they mangle spaghetti
              they give the result a mysterious Latin name.)
… But I digress; metaphorically the sausage part feeds on the strand of *fusilli*
      which becomes shorter with every bite,
          And tho' it normally takes many years to consume
              when that finally happens, it's "*Turn out the light*!?!"
When eventually all of your cooties die,
      concurrently you take your last breath.
          So the secret to longer life is to put your cooties on a diet
              so they eat more slowly but don't starve to death.
The way to achieve that, the medical scientists found, was to
      "Drink milk just *one percent* lowfat --
          If it's more than *one*, your cooties eat faster,
              and you know the unhappy outcome of that!?! "
If they'd stopped right there, we'd breathe a sigh of relief,
      knowing the key to life everlasting…
          "…By the way," they continued, "drinking *NO* milk's as bad,
              casting doubt on that one percent finding."
Did I mention medical scientists are generally assholes,
      for job security drawing conclusions inconclusive!?!
          "We're almost there, give us one more Grant,
              and by next year we'll be just as elusive!?!"

**101**

# MOMS
# &
# DADS

**Happy Mother's Day !!!**

Here's to every lady who's a Mother
       Without you there'd be neither
           a sister nor a brother.
It's incredible you have/had a baby-making
       factory in your uterus
           What a fascinating way to make
               people who are new to us.
But as you know,
       the miracle of birth is just the start
           Followed by years & years & years & years
               of Mothering with all your heart.
Watching a child learn and develop
       is truly a joy to be seen;
           Tho' "joy" has different definitions
               when he or she becomes a teen!
No matter, Moms are always there
       every step along the way,
           And tho' we celebrate you formally
               on just this special day,
You're always in our heart and soul;
       we can never thank you enough …
           …. Okay, I've got to stop now,
               this poem's making my stomach
                  feel pretty rough!?!


**Happy Father's Day !!!**

Here's to Men:
       we just stick it in,
           And thereafter
               we just play with the kid !?!
If we've done it right
       they turn out bright,
           So we just do it again and again !!

# A POEM TOO FAR?

**A Poem Too Far?**
        **or**
        **Can I Be In *The Dead Poet's Society* Now?**

I started writing this years ago        ( 12-10-10 )
       to "*en-poem*" deep thoughts I remember,
          But I dove so deep that when I awoke
             my ashes were just an ember!?!
When I began
       there was plenty of time
          to pen something truly and utterly profound;
             And here it comes now ...
                .... No wait, that was gas;
                   What a rude and disgusting sound!
Two-thousand-TBD was a wonderful year,
       ...... except for the part where I die .......
          But it's been a great ride,
             and I'm probably glad it's over
                ... give me another year and I'll try to think why.
I'd planned to live forever,
       I mostly ate twigs and dirt,
          And I exercised almost daily it seemed
             unless something came up or I hurt.
But apparently we *die* sooner or later ...
       ... and of course I was hoping for later!
          So I guess it's Plan C: ashes scattered on the ocean,
             soul riding *Up* in that Gold Elevator?
You know: you get old, your dick stops workin',
       and many other best friends are dead;
          So life's not as fun, the lust and laughter are subdued ...
             ... You think, "Why bother to get out of bed?"
I'll tell you why: it's the *Lady* on my right
       and the *Friends* and *Family* who I cherish
          ... Plus I feel a little guilty about all my stuff in the garage
             that they'll have to sort thru after I perish

And there's still a bunch to laugh at
  -- tho' it's often gallows humor --
    this one always tickles me to the max:
      A **loudly proclaimed** high frequency theory
        ... woven thru *low* frequency facts !?!
Did I mention our brains <u>love</u> to speculate,
  drawing conclusions usually optimistic?
    Yet we're always surprised
      when our schedules and costs
        are usually unrealistic!?!
Oops: I've digressed -- swerved wildly off course --
  this poem was meant to be brief,
    'Twas meant to convey ***my fondest regards for you all***;
      may joy and mirth follow this, not grief !?!
I sincerely wish you all health and happiness;
  may obstacles to your success move aside so you can pass,
    And may your automobiles need nary a single repair
      nor tires nor oil nor gas !?!
But if misfortune should somehow befall you
  -- like getting locked overnight
    with your millions of dollars in the family vault --
      Please remember I'm the one
        who wished you only good things;
          All the bad shit is somebody else's fault !!
And yes I know I've plagiarized
  from my other dittys,
    the better to complete this rhyme,
      But it saved me quite a lot of
        what I don't have any more of:
          All together now: can you say, "*Time*!?!"

## A(nother) Final Poem

Another final poem from Dave
  whose ashes were tossed upon the ocean:
    Hopefully you didn't toss your lunch too
      because of the constantly heaving wave motion !??!

**107**

www.ingramcontent.com/pod-product-compliance
Lightning Source LLC
Chambersburg PA
CBHW080939030426
42339CB00009B/475